Creative Reading

MISS EDNA STILT
of Papua
HAS NEVER READ A BOOK
IN HER LIFE, YET SHE
HAS LICKED EVERY PAGE
OF *Shakespeare's Complete
Works*

Creative Reading

What It Is, How to Do It, and Why

Ron Padgett

National Council of Teachers of English
1111 W. Kenyon Road, Urbana, Illinois 61801-1096

Permissions

Glen Baxter for his frontispiece drawing, from *The Works* (Wyrd Press, 1977). Ron Loewinsohn, for his poem "Semi-colon; for Philip Whalen" from his book *Meat Air. The New York Times* for permission to reproduce a portion of the front page of its July 6, 1986, issue, copyright © 1986 by The New York Times Co. Reprinted by permission. Judith Steinbergh and Wampeter Press for use of Ramah McKay's poem. Emmett Williams, editor of *Anthology of Concrete Poetry*, for use of Paul DeVree's poem in that collection.

Portions of this book appeared in *Teachers & Writers* magazine, Vol. 21, No. 5; *I Live to Read & Write*, Vermont Department of Education, 1991; and *Educating the Imagination*, edited by Christopher Edgar and Ron Padgett, published by Teachers & Writers Collaborative in 1994.

Manuscript Editor: Hilary Taylor Holbrook

Production Editor: Michelle Sanden Johlas

Cover Designer: Christopher Edgar

Interior Book Designer: Doug Burnett

NCTE Stock Number 09063-3050

Library of Congress Cataloging-in-Publication Data

Padgett, Ron.
     Creative reading : what it is, how to do it, and why / Ron Padgett.
       p.   cm.
     Includes bibliographical references and index.
     ISBN 0-8141-0906-3 (pbk.)
       1. Reading. 2. Creation (Literary, artistic, etc.). 3. Reading, Psychology of.
I. Title.
LB1050.2.P35   1997
372.41—dc21   96-38010

This book is dedicated,
with admiration, gratitude, and affection,
to Kenneth Koch.

Contents

Table of Figures   viii

Acknowledgments   xi

Preface   xiii

1. Taking a Ride on the Reading   1
2. My Personal History   7
3. Your Personal History   31
4. Unconscious Errors in Reading   38
5. Two Normal Eyes and Nine Everyday Mistakes   42
6. Creative Reading Techniques   56
7. Other Voices   110
8. New Reading   124
9. Reading in Unusual Situations   129
10. Other Faces   133

Appendix: Skywriting   141

Notes   145

Bibliography   149

Index   155

Author   161

Figures

1. From *Think-and-Do Book*.   9

2. The alphabet (printed).   13

3. How letters are made, using printing.   14

4. The alphabet (script).   15

5. How letters are made, using script.   16

6. From *Using Words*.   18

7. Front page of *My Weekly Reader*.   23

8. "Reading" a painting.   44

9. Trickle down example 1.   63

10. Trickle down example 2.   64

11. A "river."   65

12. Edge blur.   66

13. Two columns example.   75

14. Front page of the *New York Times*. .   76

15. Fold-in example.   84

16. Pattern for reading fold-in example in Figure 15.   85

17. Grid example.   92

18. Four reading patterns.   97

19. Spanish comic.   98

20. *Cherry* comic strip by Joe Brainard and Ron Padgett.   99

21. Cussing man.   119

22. Ron Loewinsohn poem.   120

23. Paul de Vree poem.   121

24. Apollinaire's "It's Raining" calligram.   126

25. Marinetti's "Parole in libertà."   127

26. Long lines example.   137

27. Cars at intersection.   139

Outside of a dog, reading is a man's best friend. Inside a dog it's too dark to read.

—Groucho Marx

Acknowledgments

I 'd like to thank the patient and helpful librarians at Teachers College, Columbia University; Butler Library, Columbia University; the Research Division of the New York Public Library; the Kellogg-Hubbard Library, Montpelier, Vermont; and John Donohue and the librarians at the *New Yorker*.

I owe a great debt of gratitude to others who helped me invent this book: the late John Waldman, friend and reading specialist; my colleagues over the years at Teachers & Writers Collaborative, particularly Chris Edgar; the wise editorial board of the National Council of Teachers of English; Dawn Boyer, Michelle Sanden Johlas, and Marlo Welshons, astute and cheerful editors at NCTE; my junior high school teacher Lillie Roberts, who awakened my interest in reading; my students in Imaginative Writing at Columbia University; the late Lewis Meyer, the Tulsa bookseller who showed me great kindness when I was in my teens; my friend George Schneeman for reading an early draft and helping with Italian translation; my agent Robert Cornfield; and fellow writers David Antin, Ted Berrigan, Geof Hewitt, Gary Moore, Judith Steinbergh, Tom Veitch, James Wanless, Emmett Williams, and Larry Zirlin. I also thank my friend Glen Baxter for use of his drawing as a frontispiece, and fellow poet Ron Loewinsohn for use of his poem "Semicolon; for Philip Whalen." I hope that some of the joy of having collaborated with artist Joe Brainard is evident in our comic strip in this book. Most of all, I thank my wife Patricia, *sine qua non*.

Preface

A few years ago, it struck me that I couldn't remember ever having learned to read. How *had* I learned? How do others learn to read? How would I teach someone else? The more I thought about reading, the more it seemed a kind of miracle, and it was my growing fascination with this miracle that led me to examine my ideas about it. At a certain point, I saw that these ideas led to a particular approach, which I've called creative reading, a corollary to creative writing.

In this book, I define creative reading, tell how to do it and why. I discuss various types of reading errors and tell how to capitalize on them. The most experimental parts of the book (Chapters 6 and 7) present specific methods and exercises for creative reading, exercises involving classic and modern literature, writing, listening, thinking, teaching, and learning. I offer ways to retrace your own reading history, so you can see what has made you the kind of reader you are. To make doing so easier, I summarize the principal methods of reading instruction in American schools during the past 75 years. Along the way, I also discuss, among other things, the role of the unconscious in reading, intentional mishearing, the music of Spike Jones, skywriting, Dada poetry, and time travel.

Perhaps I should say a few words about what this book *doesn't* intend to do. It doesn't tell how to teach beginners to read. It doesn't comprehensively survey the vast literature of the pedagogy of reading. And although many of its ideas are practical, it does not propose a formal "method." It is the view of a poet who prefers ideas and images when they first materialize, still trailing clouds of mystery, before the life gets squeezed out of them by codification. It is a book either for people who have learned to read—perhaps even well—in conventional ways, but who sense a creeping staleness in their reading, or for those who have a taste for literary adventure. It is emphatically not an attack on conventional reading, nor is it an outgrowth of deconstruction, an intellectual trend that I heard of long after I had formed the ideas I present here.

The general aim of the book is simply to enlarge the possibilities of reading, by demonstrating ways to make reading more flexible, various, and imaginative, and by suggesting a new, more inventive attitude toward the act of reading. This new attitude is one that encourages the integration of reading and writing. In fact, the book's underlying assumption is that reading and writing should be seen as two sides of the same coin, not as disciplines connected only by the fact that both use words.

That's what happens too often in school: we have our students study reading for a while, then close their books and work on spelling, grammar, and punctuation. What's worse, we administer standardized tests that purport to measure progress in quantitative terms. All too often, the test scores become more important than what they were meant to measure, and we begin to "teach for the test." At the same time, we break down reading and writing into smaller units, known as "skills." The skills approach has been characterized as the "closed" system, best understood if contrasted with the "open" system (Lee and Allen 4–5). In the open system, reading instruction begins with the learner's recognition that his or her own talk can be put into written form; in the closed system, the learner begins with learning to read print. In the open system, reading is integrated with writing, and the instruction honors the students' interests; in the closed, the emphasis is on a preset sequence of reading skills established by reading experts. In the open system, students' progress is measured by students' enthusiasm for reading and self-expression; in the closed, by standardized tests. And so on.

Skills and drills go hand in hand with achievement tests. The trouble with the skills approach is that it is boring and artificial. It makes reading and writing harder to learn—and far less enjoyable—than they should be. If we were taught to talk the way we're taught to read, most of us would be mute.

On top of it all, for more than 20 years we have had "experts" telling us that we as a nation are "at risk" because our students don't do well enough on tests:

> International comparisons of student achievement. . . reveal that on 19 academic tests American students were never first or second and, in comparison with other industrialized nations, were last seven times. (National Commission on Excellence in Education 6)

This failure poses a threat to "American prosperity, security, and civility" (5), presumably in that order. We haven't even competed well against ourselves. According to one reading expert, "SAT (Scholastic Aptitude Test) scores, particularly the verbal scores, have declined steadily from 1967 to 1980," then levelled off (Chall, *Stages* 6). By 1992, among 17-year-olds the average proficiency in reading had risen slightly, but among college-bound twelfth graders, the level was still well below that of 1972 (Smith et al. 68; National Center for Education Statistics 113).

If poor test scores mean that children are reading less and less well, we should be alarmed. It's a serious matter. But what do we mean by "reading less and less well"? And why do we always hear government officials, social workers, and even educators telling us that a good education is important because it enables us to get a "better job"? Such a statement is not simply an exhortation to the potential high school dropout. It exemplifies a philosophy of life. *A Nation at Risk* treats reading and other academic subjects as if they were forms of the gross national product. But do we always learn to read and write and compute primarily to get a better job? What is a "better" job? One with more money, more prestige, more security? And do we teach our children to read mainly so they can get a "higher" score or a "better" grade—that is, to "succeed"? If we do, we forget the point of learning, and there is something lacking: *quality of life*. In terms of reading, what is lacking is the warmth of learning about the world, other people, and oneself, of learning to live more fully and variously, with greater understanding, clarity, and compassion, as well as beauty and good humor.

I'm not quite brazen enough to promise that this book will put anyone in immediate possession of these qualities, but my hope is that it will set us off in their general direction.

1 Taking a Ride on the Reading

My beloved put in his hand by the hole of the door, and my bowels were moved for him.

—Song of Solomon, 5:4, King James Version

I remember, in playing the game of Monopoly as a child, picking up a Chance card, the one that depicted the mustachioed gentleman in top hat and tails astride a locomotive, alongside the instruction, "Take a ride on the Reading." Those words would induce in me the momentary feeling that this railway (pronounced "Redding") had something to do with books—perhaps a mobile library. Like many such misunderstandings, this one had its particular moment of crazy wisdom: one of the great joys of books is the way they transport us, through space and time. We take a ride on the reading.

I also misunderstood the title of Oscar Wilde's poem "The Ballad of Reading Gaol." In addition to *reading*, it has the additional problem of *gaol,* which I thought sounded like "gale" spoken in a strong southern accent. When I learned it was pronounced "jail," I still misunderstood the title, fearing that it referred to a penal institution for bad readers. These unfortunates would be sent to Reading Jail, while the gifted would take a ride on the Reading.*

English abounds with such pitfalls of misunderstanding, some of which, such as the biblical quotation at the start of this chapter, can be quite funny. It is amazing that non-English-speaking people learn to speak and read English as well as they do. Growing up in America, I found nothing odd in the fact that *rough* was pronounced "ruff," and that adding a *th* in front of it changed the whole thing to "throo." The rules of English phonetics and spelling are riddled with exceptions. Such nooks and crannies

---

*Even the big computerized catalog of the New York Public Library confuses the various meanings of "reading." In doing research for this book, I asked the computer to list every new book (since 1972) on the subject of reading. It listed 684 items, including studies of Reading, Pennsylvania, mind reading, and Reading, England. What appeared to be a history of reading (*Reading As It Was*) turned out to be a history of the American city. One title was particularly intriguing: *The Library That Would Not Die: The Turbulent History of the Reading Public Library*.

of a language, such fickleness and variability, such trap doors, such odd moments in what otherwise appears to be a consistent system—these are the monkey wrenches that give languages something of a human caste, a fallibility. We forgive our language for these "flaws," just as we hope we can be forgiven for our lack of mastery over it.

But the idea of "mastery" dominates our language instruction. The decades continue to roll by with school texts and drill books with titles along the lines of *Mastering English, Drills to Ensure Mastery*, and *Mastering the Skills of Reading*, all providing us with "word-attack skills." Such titles suggest that the teacher is a drill sergeant and the students are little recruits who must be regimented into the proper patterns of phonics, word recognition, and comprehension, who must be taught to sound off properly.

Researchers in reading instruction have gone (and continue to go) to great lengths to learn what reading is, why some learn to do it well and others don't, and what are the best ways to teach all our children to read. Since the turn of the century, this research has led to interesting discoveries, but too often, by the time the research filters down into the classroom, it has been made into a rigid system that nullifies much of its initial value.

Constance Weaver identifies six approaches to the teaching of reading: the phonics approach, the linguistics approach, the "look–say" approach, the basal reader approach, the language experience approach, and the whole language approach (4–46). To my thinking and in my experience, the whole language approach makes the most sense by far, but even whole language, that most generous of approaches, can become formulaic and mechanistic in the hands of a cold or narrow-minded teacher. And any approach—especially an approach that isn't very warm in the first place—can be dehumanized by a zealot. Phonics zombies are particularly scary.

The coldest of all instruments in the teaching of reading is the test. For some time now, the effectiveness of reading instruction has been measured by methods that yield quantitative results: a child can be tested and said to be reading below, at, or above grade level. Although such tests can do what they set out to do, they can also be misleading or even highly pernicious.

There is something missing in most of the research and commentary on reading and in the way reading is taught: a quirky, private, creative, playful, and even wilfull streak that runs through us all, a part of ourselves that quietly but steadily goes about remaking the world to suit ourselves.

Artists and creative thinkers nurture this part of themselves. (Poet Dick Higgins even founded an Institute for Creative Misunderstanding.) It is the element in us that corresponds to those·odd moments when the rules of our language temporarily break down, those organic, surprising, confusing twists that make words so free, as if they had a will of their own.

It is generally conceded that creativity in writing is a good thing. In our universities, we now have what amounts to a creative writing industry; it is possible to obtain a master's degree in poetry writing. Many high schools offer courses in creative writing. Creative writing is now a regular part of countless elementary school curricula. As a writer who has taught poetry writing to children and teachers, I think this is wonderful for many reasons, not the least of which is that creative writing helps people take charge of themselves, to be less passive.

Writing is considered to be an active activity. In this essentially true but oversimplified view, the words flow from the writer out onto the paper. Writers know, however, that what really happens is that the words originate either inside or outside the writer, go into the writer's conscious mind, move out onto the paper, and then affect what words come next, forming a kind of rolling cycle. For example, I just wrote the word *cycle,* and for an instant I had an image of the Harley-Davidson motorcycle my father rode as a young man. Normally, this image would have been only vaguely sensed and certainly not mentioned, but it would have affected what I wrote next, possibly a reminiscence of my childhood. I might have gone on to discuss how I learned to write, what it was like being in the first grade in 1948, and so on. The point here is that writing is not unidirectional, from the writer out; it is at least bidirectional, both out and in at the same time. It is like a conversation, but with oneself. In any case, writing is fundamentally active.

Reading, in the oversimplified view, is seen as comparatively passive: the words travel from the page (or screen or whatever) and into us, who sit there receiving. We allow the words to light up certain areas of the brain, to revive memories, to create scenes and excite emotions, even to make us wonder, but in some fundamental way, we are under the control of the words coming in. Sometimes we have to work to interpret them, but they have a sovereignty that makes them inviolate to our tampering.

Louise Rosenblatt describes the act of reading as intrinsically active. She views it as a transaction between reader and text, in which the reader participates in the creation of the work of literature, which by definition is different for each reader, and even for the same reader at different times. Her view, which makes perfect sense to me, echoes one expressed by Fernando Pessoa in his *Book of Disquiet*:

> I have never been able to read a single book to which I give myself over entirely; at each step, always, the incessant commentary of intelligence and imagination interrupted the thread of the narrative. After a few minutes, it was I who was writing the book—and what I wrote nowhere existed. (57)

Most readers seem to feel that they have the opposite experience, in which reader and author remain distinct and separate, and the printed word radiates an unassailable aura of power. An essay in print feels far more authoritative than the same essay in typescript. Every time a manuscript I have edited is set in type, I say to myself, "This stuff is even better than I thought!" Bind it in hardcover: it looks even more imposing. Call it something like *The Oxford Book of Reading* and it takes on an even greater aura of authority. *Imprimatur.**

From an early age, we are instilled with respect for the printed word. Those of us who, for some reason or another, do not learn to read easily can begin to resent this obligatory respect, while fast learners, rewarded for their facility, feed more and more off their own success, increasing their respect for the system of printed words that is so gratifying to them. In the former case, the child doesn't learn to read well or at all, and at an early age is defeated by reading: it is too difficult to master, too powerful. In the latter case, the child can begin to worship that same power. Whether feared or revered, the printed word emerges as powerful.

Infants love to make marks on paper (and walls)—pencil marks, felt-tip pen marks, crayon marks. If they see older children and adults writing, they too will "write" by making scribble marks. Sometimes they will draw a picture and scribble a caption below it. You can't read their writing, for it belongs to no known system of writing, but they can. They will tell you that it means that "the horse is taking a nap," for instance. They go to school taking pleasure in their writing. Then things begin to change.

They learn that there is a right way and a wrong way. They learn that there are rules, and the rules have to be learned. They become more aware of their classmates, whose esteem they want and with whom they feel they must compete. Their writing is graded. The teacher marks the mistakes on their papers. They realize that their handwriting is faulty, their spelling is terrible, that no matter how hard they try, they will never,

---

*Referring to detective novels, though, writer and artist Joe Brainard said, "Some books are *better* in paperback."

ever write a perfect essay. Their writing cries out for improvement. Even those who go on to college will do so hating the dreaded term paper, the essay question, the book report, any form of writing that requires more than a true-false or multiple-choice response. This attitude explains why their writing improves so slowly, and why so few adults outside of school write anything at all: no one wants to produce something they will see only as flawed. Why bother?

Reading is a different matter. Printed words seem perfect. Think back to when you were little, struggling to spell words such as "cat." Can you remember how awesome the big words looked then? I can remember thinking that "antidisestablishmentarianism" was the longest word in the world and therefore one that could be spelled only by a genius. (It still looks pretty impressive, for an English word, like a battleship gliding slowly into an estuary.) Can you remember ever seeing a misspelling in a school reader or textbook? They must be few and far between. Furthermore, the schoolbooks are the ones that are laying down the law to us, so it is natural for us to assume that they know what they're talking about. The rules of reading and writing are set out in sober black ink on no-nonsense white paper, which confirms their authority. Printed words are never wrong.

"How do you know?"

"I read it in a book."

Or:

"Look, let's settle this question once and for all. Let's call the library."

Of course books are filled with all sorts of great information and misinformation, and reading is more than the receiving of information. The point here is that printed words have such authority that they seem chiseled in stone. We are rarely, if ever, taught that printed words might be changed, played with, bounced around, or cut in half: in short, that we could read as actively as we write, that we could read *creatively*. This lack of permission—and of techniques for doing so once permission is granted—may prove to have been a barrier to our learning how to bring more of ourselves to what we read. We may have been reading all these years with only half a brain.

Creative Reading explores this other side of reading, presents some methods of reading creatively, and explains how they work and why. It grew out of years of wondering why I—a writer—hadn't been taking greater pleasure in reading. My friends were always raving about some "wonderful" book they were reading, a book I was "sure to love." Every once in a great while they were right, but all too often I'd trot back from the bookstore or library with said treasure in hand, only to find, part way through it, that it was not as advertised. I wouldn't know whether to blame my friends or myself. It just seemed that I didn't get deeply absorbed in reading, I didn't find myself reading in great long lost stretches of time, I wasn't getting enough nourishment from what I read. If my eyes strayed from the printed page over to the window, I found the view outside much more satisfying: I preferred "reading" the cornice against the blue sky across the street. Surely there was something wrong with me. Why didn't I like to read more? If there was a problem, it must have its origin in the past, perhaps in my childhood. Had I been taught to read in the wrong way? My autobiographical inquiry eventually led me to realize that such inquiry could be interesting for others to pursue, too.

2 My Personal History

The bear the lion the chimpanzee the rattlesnake taught me how to read.

—Blaise Cendrars

I started at the beginning, trying to recall my first experiences with reading. I naively hoped that I would be able to recall my first encounter with a letter of the alphabet. Under hypnosis, I tried to regress to that first letter. My quest for this primal alphabetical experience was misguided, because the memory of such an experience would have been transformed again and again by subsequent experiences with the alphabet. It would have become a memory of a memory of a memory of a memory etc. of an experience, with the experience so many steps removed, altered by each removal, unrecoverable in its pure state. It was like trying to understand a tree by first studying an electron of a seed. Likewise, I doubt that I will ever be able to recall recognizing and reading those initial words such as *daddy*, *cat*, and *no*.

Hypnosis was helpful, though, in opening up old memory cells in the brain. It helped me remember being able to read comic books (called "funny books" in Oklahoma, where I grew up, in the 1940s) before I ever attended school. My mother claims that one day I started reading all by myself. Of course this just doesn't happen: she or others had shown me, inadvertently perhaps, which way books are held, in which direction the pages are read, that the black marks represent words, that written words have sounds, that in comic books the words go with pictures in the same frame, and so on. Of course, the pictures showed me which way was right-side-up. What my mother meant is that she didn't formally instruct me. She read to me, no doubt with her finger skimming along under the words and then pointing to the pictures, and I began to recognize certain simple words. There came, though, a magic moment when it all jelled, and I could read "by myself." It doesn't matter that I skipped some of the words and misread others: the whole act of reading by myself made sense. Learning to read was like learning to ride a bicycle. My father ran alongside the bike, pushing and holding it steady until—bingo—I wobbled off down the street by myself. Years later, when I asked him about it, he groaned about having to propel me around the house, day after day, until he was about to drop. The funny thing is that I recall his doing it only a few minutes before I took off on my own. It's likely that my impression of my mother's reading to me only a few times is equally foreshortened.

I also learned to read by riding in a car. My parents took great pride in their cars, keeping them clean, polished, and serviced. Like many other families in those days, we would sometimes simply go out for a ride. In *All about Our Baby*, our family baby album, my mother wrote that by the age of one, I "liked to ride in car an awful lot." By the time I was five, I could identify every make of car on the road. It seems to me that children in the 1940s were excited to go riding in a car; they looked eagerly out the window a lot more than children do now. (Now children look *in* the TV window.) When I was a preschooler, one of my favorite things to do in a car was to read the signs. "STOP" was a natural, as were "EAT," "GAS," and "HAMBURGERS." Equally compelling and not much more difficult for me was the cool blue neon that spelled out "MORRIS'S SUNDRY STORE," my prime source of funny books and chocolate malts. And later, when we drove down Route 66 to Texas to visit my aunt, I read signs along the way: "El Reno," "Elk City," "Sayre," "Welcome to Texas," "Shamrock," "Amarillo." And all along, my mother, without knowing it, was teaching me to read.

After I started school, she let the teachers handle my reading. Reading instruction began, in the first grade, with the Scott, Foresman basic reader and workbook program, better known as "Dick and Jane." These readers have long since been rightly excoriated for their narrow images of race and class, but they seem to me to have been well-thought-out for teaching some basic concepts of reading.

Notice that I said teaching *concepts*. Look at Figure 1. It shows a page from my workbook that went with one of the first readers, *We Look and See*. The page's four panels show Dick playing with his toy train. Each panel contains a caption. The note to the teacher explains that the aim of this exercise is to "promote the ability to interpret a picture-story sequence; to give practice in associating pictures and text; to give practice in comparing one-line reading units of familiar words." Already a devourer of comic books whose narratives and panels were far more complex and interesting than those of "Dick and Jane," I had no trouble fulfilling the first two stated aims. The third aim seems to have eluded me at panel three, where I neglected to underline any of the phrases (perhaps because the identical phrases were not consecutive, as they were in the other three panels). I finished the exercise by coloring in Dick's shirt and the train.

I find it hard to imagine what *reading* pleasure I could have gotten from such materials. I got pleasure from completing an assigned task; I got pleasure from being praised for doing so; and I got pleasure from the challenges in problem-solving that such workbooks presented. But I did

Figure 1. From *Think-and-Do Book*.

not get pleasure in reading, because the subject matter, compared to that of *Plastic Man* or even *Nancy & Sluggo*, was less than pedestrian. The narrative anemia of the Dick and Jane scenarios caused the words to lose their interest. I learned the words and did the exercises, but not because they excited or engaged me. I did them because the teacher told me to. Thus, for the first time, my reading became disconnected from my real interests. Reading became a part of my school life and my school self, and when I went home at the end of the day I pretty much left that self at school, preferring instead to play or daydream or listen to radio serials (and a few years later, to watch television). I don't think my experience of disconnected reading is all that different from those of my classmates then, or from those of many kids today.

My teachers used a combination of what reading specialists call word recognition and phonics. Here is the gist of each method. With word recognition, the teacher shows the child a word and says it aloud: "cat." The child learns to recognize the word as a whole. With phonics, the student learns how individual letters usually sound, so he or she can "sound out" the letters and blend them into words: "c-a-t." Both methods have variations and sophistications, described by Jeanne S. Chall in her study, *Learning to Read: The Great Debate*.

According to Chall, the phonics method of instruction was dominant during the period 1890–1920. From 1920 to 1935, schools emphasized the word recognition method. From 1935 to 1955, the phonics method made a gradual return. Of course, these trends affected some parts of the country more than others, some types of schools (parochial, public) more than others, some teachers (new, veteran, rigid, experimental, etc.) more than others. It is probable that an inflexible, veteran teacher in a small, conservative town still would have been teaching phonics until 1935, that is, straight through the word recognition period. My wife was first taught to read in 1943 in a parochial school that used the word recognition method. Only a few blocks away and five years later, I was taught to read in a public school that combined phonics and word recognition. My school's approach was probably that of William S. Gray, described by Jeanne Chall as the "acknowledged leader of, and spokesman for, reading experts for four decades; major summarizer and interpreter of research; and author of America's leading basal-reader series" (Chall, *Learning to Read*, 96). He advocated a sight-recognition-first, phonics-later approach.

The combined approach was the result of the work of many researchers and teachers, all trying their hardest to figure out the best way to teach children to read.[1] The combination of look–say and phonics methods has its virtues, but it doesn't go far enough. It failed, in my case and in many others', not because I didn't learn to read, but because I didn't learn to love to read. The authors of "Dick and Jane" and other basic readers seemed to have had no idea what might interest a child. The "Dick and Jane" authors' claim, that the *Think-and-Do Book* "contains much new and interesting reading material to . . . contribute to [the student's] enjoyment of the new experience of reading," rings utterly hollow (Gray and Monroe, inside front cover).

Much the same can be said about instruction in writing, despite several encouraging trends—writers-in-the-schools, the use of the "writing process," and whole language—over the past few decades. At the same time as we are taught to read in school, we are taught to write. It is possible, of course, to learn to read without learning to write; without being able to form a single letter of the alphabet, toddlers can learn to read at a very early age.[2] But there is no doubt that reading and writing reinforce each other, just as reading silently and reading aloud reinforce each other. But when writing is taught poorly, the effect of the reinforcement is negative. Dismal writing assignments that parallel dismal reading matter send too many students away from school convinced that the last thing they want to do is read or write. They come to see reading and writing as boring work, and boring work is hard to do, and when it is forced on students, they feel crushed, defeated, resentful, apathetic, or guilty. These reactions reflect many students' sense of failure and weakness: the written word is just too difficult, too powerful for them to handle.[3]

When I was learning to write, my teachers put a great premium on penmanship. In the first grade, we were shown how to print. We used wide-ruled paper whose solid light-blue lines were divided in half by dotted lines to help us proportion the letters. I liked learning to print. I liked the way the letters looked when they were formed neatly, and for some reason I enjoyed trying to make the unattainable, perfect O. The only thing I didn't like was getting writer's cramp, and having the pencil make a dent in the middle finger of my writing hand. I had never had dents in my body before, and at first I wasn't sure they would go away. We wrote with extra-thick Laddy pencils. I've always wondered why children with small hands were given such an unwieldy instrument. In any case, our penmanship drills consisted of copying the individual letters over and over, until we learned them.

The same materials were used in teaching us to write script: in our case, a variant of the Palmer Method. Script, with its slanted letters and curlicues, seemed less visually attractive to me, but it was faster, and it had a more grown-up feel to it—"little" kids didn't know how to do it. The rules for the formation of the letters in script were exact, and the teachers marked off for any variation. We were never told that this was just one system among many—that handwriting styles come and go—so that when I first saw reproductions of the Declaration of Independence and The Bill of Rights, I suspected that our founding fathers had been weird, perhaps un-American, so crazed, bizarre, and illegible did their handwriting look. Nor were we told that handwriting varied from country to country. Asian calligraphy was so far off the graph that it was never even mentioned. Handwriting was presented as a monolithic set of rules: you do it *this* way, and that's all there is to it. (See Figures 2–5, which show the flyleaf pages, front and back of *Using Words*, my second-grade spelling textbook.)

We were also given the impression that punctuation had existed from time immemorial. It took me about 30 years to ask myself, "Who invented the question mark?" It turns out that our system of punctuation has been in effect for only around 400 years. In ancient Greece, for instance, the words tended to be run together with virtually no punctuation, though there were paragraph divisions. Occasionally, there was *some* punctuation: in a third-century B.C. text, for instance, the double point (:) served as a period. The single point, placed high on the line, also indicated a period. The same point, placed in the middle of the line, indicated a comma. "Our" comma appeared around the ninth century. But it wasn't until the end of the fifteenth century and the beginning of the sixteenth that our system of word separation and punctuation was standardized.[4]

Even the pronunciation of the alphabet has changed. Until the last century, we Americans called the *z* in the British manner ("zed"). We also concluded the recitation of the alphabet by saying ". . . x, y, z and per se and." The *per se and* indicated the symbol &, now called the "ampersand."[5] Nowadays we say "zee" and don't include the ampersand. My teachers always gave the impression that punctuation and the alphabet were absolute and unchanging.

It was the same with spelling. There was no sense that any word had ever been spelled any differently from the way we were being taught to spell it—these words were cut in stone in the great dictionary of eternity. They never had been any different and they never would be, and if we didn't learn to spell them correctly, we would be deemed ignorant and unkempt forever, like the boy in our school who arrived each morning with his hair askew and his shirttail hanging out on one side. My teachers seemed not to have known that Shakespeare and his contemporaries used variant spellings of even their own names.

Although researchers have found that there is no correlation between spelling ability and general intelligence—not to mention greatness:

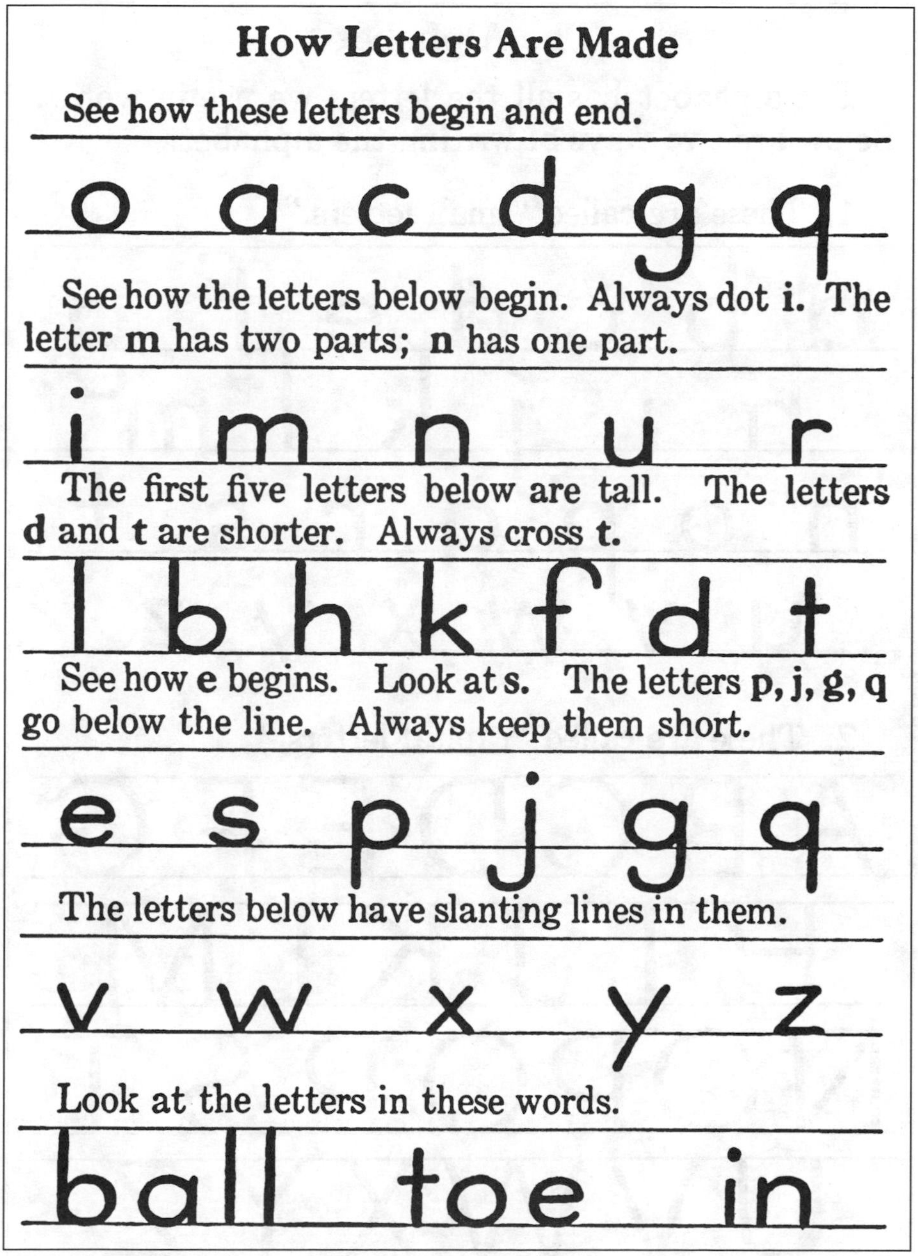

How Letters Are Made

See how these letters begin and end.

o a c d g q

See how the letters below begin. Always dot **i**. The letter **m** has two parts; **n** has one part.

i m n u r

The first five letters below are tall. The letters **d** and **t** are shorter. Always cross **t**.

l b h k f d t

See how **e** begins. Look at **s**. The letters **p, j, g, q** go below the line. Always keep them short.

e s p j g q

The letters below have slanting lines in them.

v w x y z

Look at the letters in these words.

ball toe in

Figure 2. The alphabet (printed).

The Alphabet

The alphabet has all the letters we use in words. Below are two ways of writing the alphabet.

1. These are called "small letters."

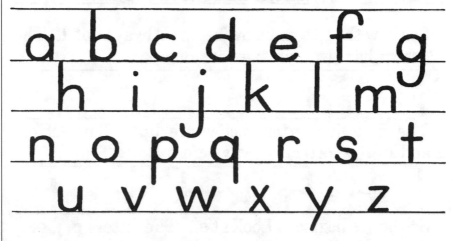

2. These are called "capital letters."

Figure 3. How letters are made, using printing.

The Alphabet

The alphabet has all the letters we use in words. Below are two ways of writing the alphabet.

1. These are called "small letters."

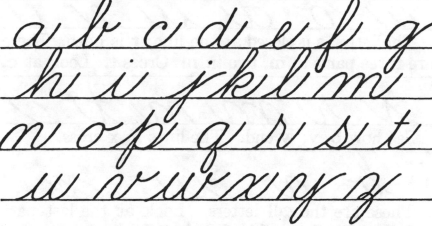

2. These are called "capital letters."

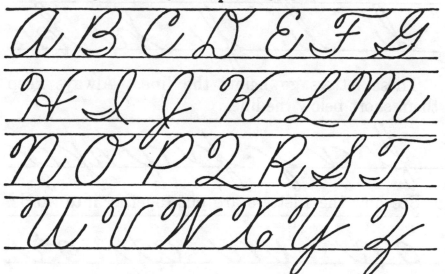

Figure 4. The alphabet (script).

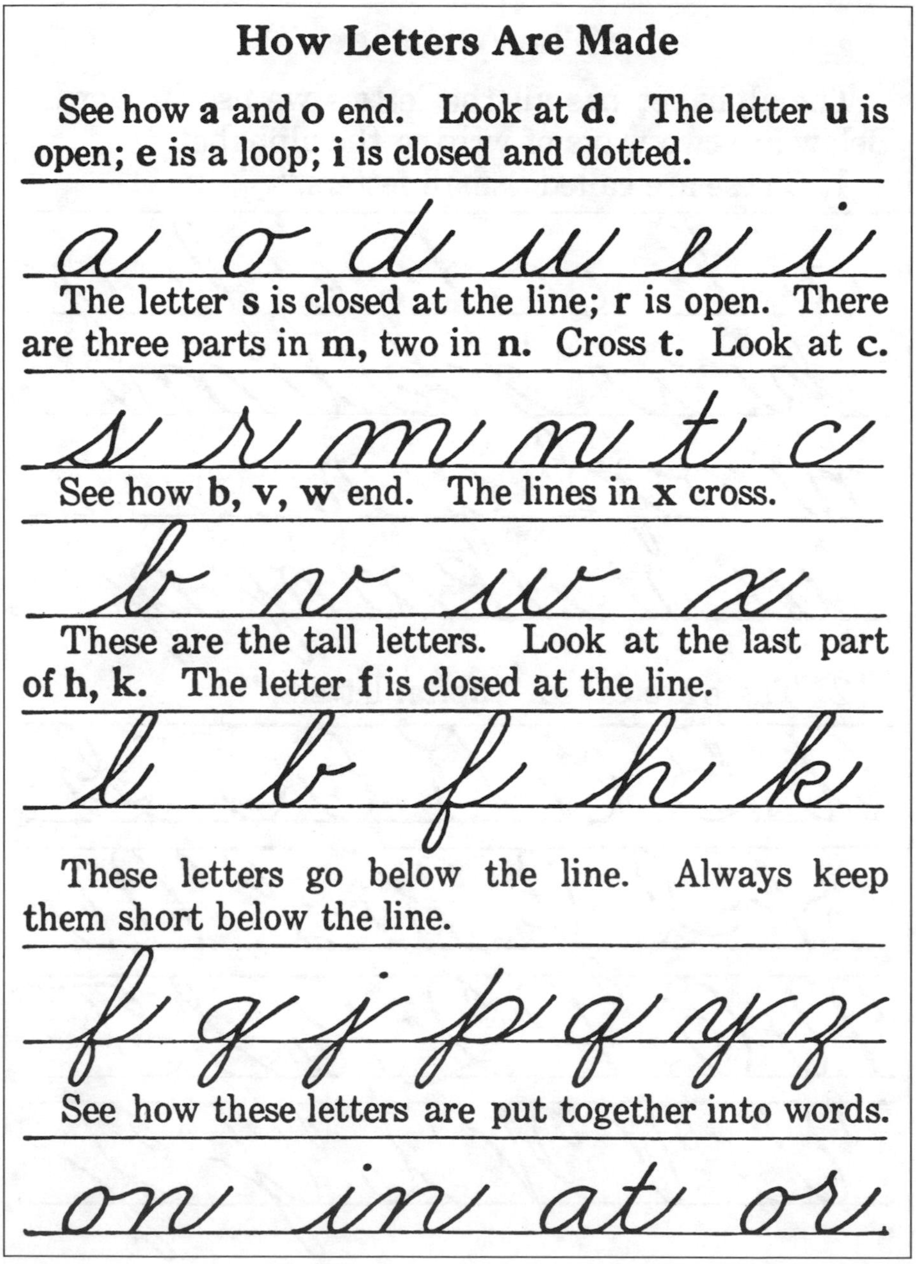

How Letters Are Made

See how **a** and **o** end. Look at **d**. The letter **u** is open; **e** is a loop; **i** is closed and dotted.

a   o   d   u   e   i

The letter **s** is closed at the line; **r** is open. There are three parts in **m**, two in **n**. Cross **t**. Look at **c**.

s   r   m   n   t   c

See how **b, v, w** end.   The lines in **x** cross.

b   v   w   x

These are the tall letters. Look at the last part of **h, k**. The letter **f** is closed at the line.

l   b   f   h   k

These letters go below the line. Always keep them short below the line.

f   g   j   p   q   y   z

See how these letters are put together into words.

on   in   at   or

Figure 5. How letters are made, using script.

Beethoven, Yeats, and Shaw were poor spellers—my teachers still placed a great premium on correct spelling. To conform to the standards of orthography, by the third grade we were required to learn to spell 10 to 15 new words per week. On Monday, the teacher would write the new words on the board, and we would copy them on our notebook paper. Through the week, the words would be pronounced, defined, and copied over and over, in preparation for the weekly Friday test. Words misspelled on the test would have to be copied over and over and over, until it was hard to get them wrong. This was similar to using writing as a form of punishment, as in having students stay after school and write 100 times, "I will not talk in class."

A similar week-by-week system can be seen in *Using Words: An Enriched Spelling Program (Second Year)* (See Figure 6 a–d). In this program, a "story" is followed by a list of "new" words and instructions on what to do with them. In the first place, it's stretching a definition to call the collection of sentences about Dan, Spot, and Dad a "story." By grade two, most children have a much fuller and more interesting idea of what a story is. In the second place, the words *dog*, *in*, *at*, *me*, and *it* are hardly new. It's patronizing to call them "new" words when most kids will have been using them since long before they started school. And what makes them "your" new words? I never wanted them. It's like being given a pair of brown socks at Christmas. Thanks a lot.

But there's more. On the second day, we got to have "Fun with [Our] New Words." Authors of textbooks such as these have always had the most peculiar sense of what might be "fun" for a child. Students know this isn't "fun," and it's irksome to be told that it is fun. But the teacher and the textbook have authority, because they possess knowledge, and this knowledge is a source of power that children want, too. So, in response to number 1 under "Fun with Your New Words," we would write the word *dog* and tell ourselves that, well, that was *sort of* not un-fun. Especially if we got it right and the teacher praised us.

If we didn't, we had to enter the incorrect word into what the textbook author called "My Own Word Book." What a backward idea, to give the students the words they can't spell, all for their very own! Who would want such troublesome words, such a collection of personal failures? It's like giving someone an album filled with unflattering photographs of themselves. Something to keep alongside the brown socks.

I suspect that one learns to spell correctly not by doing exercises, but by reading, reading, and reading words that are spelled correctly, until the eye automatically recognizes and can confirm whether or not a word

I. Spot

Some dogs like to swim.   Dan has a little dog called Spot.   Spot likes to swim in the pond near the barn.

One day Dan said, "Look at Spot, Father. He will bring my ball to me."

Dan threw his ball into the pond.   Spot jumped into the water.   He got the ball and took it to Dan.

Your New Words

dog   in   at   me   it

First Day

1. Read the story.   Your teacher will help you.

2. Your teacher will say Your New Words. Look at each word and say it after her.

3. Find each of Your New Words in the story.   Write each word on a piece of paper.

[2]

Figure 6a. From *Using Words.*

II. Fun with Your New Words

Second Day

In this week's work Fun with Your New Words has five parts. Whenever you do Fun with Your New Words, always write the number of each part on your paper.

1. Look at the picture. Write the name of the animal beside number 1 on your paper.

2. In Your New Words find the word that sounds like **pin.** Write it beside number 2 on your paper.

3. Beside number 3 on your paper write the word that sounds like **cat.**

4. Beside number 4 write the word that begins with **m.**

5. Beside number 5 write the word that sounds like **sit.**

[3]

Figure 6b.

III. Testing Yourself

Third Day

1. Count Your New Words. Number one line on your paper for each new word.

2. Your teacher will say each of Your New Words. Write each new word beside a number.

3. Lay your paper beside your book. Look at Your New Words in your book. (In this lesson Your New Words were **dog, in, at, me, it.**) If you missed a word, draw a line through it on your paper. Write it again beside the word that is wrong. Spell it right. Save your paper.

IV. Studying the Words You Missed

Fourth Day

Look at the paper you saved. Yesterday you crossed out each word you missed. Study the words you missed. This is the way to study a word:

1. Look at the word in Your New Words. Say it to yourself. Say each letter in the word. Close your eyes and say each letter.

2. Look at the word again.

[4]

Figure 6c.

3. Write the word without looking at Your New Words. Then look at Your New Words. See if you spelled the word right.

4. Cover the word and write it again.
Do this until you can spell the word right.

V. Testing Yourself Again

Fifth Day

1. Your teacher will tell you how to number your paper.

2. Your teacher will say each of Your New Words. Write each word beside a number.

3. Look at Your New Words. Put a check like this (**X**) on your paper beside each word you missed. Your score is the number of words you spelled right. Write your score.

Making a Word Book

Your teacher will help you make a little book. You will use it every week. Print "My Own Word Book" and your name on the cover.

If you missed any words in your test, write them in MY OWN WORD BOOK. Above the words write "Week 1."

[5]

Figure 6d.

is spelled correctly. Better to spend valuable school time in meaningful and enjoyable reading than in tedious and disconnected drills.

So that our spelling words would have at least *some* relation to something other than themselves, we were required to use them in sentences, one sentence for each new word. Along with the perennial "How I Spent My Summer Vacation," this exercise was the only "creative" writing we were assigned. Except, of course, that it wasn't very creative. We weren't encouraged to invent; nor were we discouraged. We were just told to use each word in a sentence. So, to discharge the obligation, I usually wrote brief and acceptable sentences. "America is a great *country*." "I like *cereal*." "Be very *careful*." "*Tables* are very useful." The sentences were unrelated, except in their brevity and blandness. We were never told, for example, to use all the new words in a story or paragraph, as is sometimes done now; that would have forced us to be inventive, and invention was not what school was about. It was about learning rules and following them, or suffering the consequences.

But if school held the threat of punishment over us, it also held out the carrot of pleasure, albeit a rather withered carrot. Such had not always been the case. Early American primers contained material that children *ought* to know, much of it from adult sources, such as the Bible. Gradually, schoolbooks became more and more "child-centered," in an attempt to appeal to students.

Our school "reading material" was child-centered, but it always seemed to have been prepared on an erroneous assumption of what children like. For example, despite an occasionally amusing cartoon or interesting story, *My Weekly Reader*, subtitled *The Children's Newspaper*, routinely carried articles such as the one in Figure 7 that concludes, "Children are proud of their new schools." Excuse me? There was little in our school reading to inspire wonder or stir the imagination, for we were not learning to think, we were receiving an indoctrination in how we were to behave and *what* we were to think. Brought up in a family that lived in some measure by its own standards, I found such "reading material" numbing, goody-goody, and preachy, but my desire to succeed in school caused me to repress my antipathy. I read what I was supposed to, but, aside from comic books, not much else.

This is partly why I missed out on "children's literature." I didn't read nursery rhymes, fairy tales, or traditional stories. I didn't read Andersen, Perreault, or the Brothers Grimm. I didn't read the "modern classics," such as *Charlotte's Web* or the *Oz* books. I didn't even read the Hardy Boys. What I knew of children's literature was through retellings in comic books, records, animated cartoons, and Walt Disney films.

EDITION NUMBER TWO · Vol. XIX · Week of May 22-26, 1950 · No. 34

My Weekly Reader

THE CHILDREN'S NEWSPAPER

Some Children Have New Schools

This new schoolroom is light and cheerful.

The "blackboard" in this new school is green.

Some boys and girls go to school in new buildings.

The new schools have big windows. The rooms are light and cheerful. The walls are painted pretty colors. The floors are colored, too.

The rooms are big. Children have lots of room for work and play.

In some places, workmen make old schools look like new. They make dark rooms bright and cheerful.

Children are proud of their new schools.

ATTENTION PLEASE: Because of the railroad strike, the last two issues of *My Weekly Reader* have been delayed in reaching you. This is the last issue for this year.

Figure 7. Front page of *My Weekly Reader*.

The only three books I can remember owning were a novel by Fran Striker called something like *The Lone Ranger and the Lost City of Gold*; a turn-of-the-century dog novel called *Bob, Son of Battle,* by Alfred Ollivant; and *The Mickey Mantle Story*, which was one of those "as told to" jobs.

I think I read the Lone Ranger novel partly because I associated the characters with their movie and TV incarnations. Clayton Moore and Jay Silverheels, who played the Lone Ranger and Tonto (Spanish for "stupid"), had distinctive voices. Especially Silverheels. So for me, the dialogue in the novel was a breeze. It was as if the characters were reading their lines aloud to me.[6] This type of reading could have been a nice transitional stage between my being a lukewarm reader and becoming an avid one, but things didn't turn out that way. Not only did I need more sustained encouragement to read, I needed better stories. This Lone Ranger story, one in what must have been a long, tired series, was very thin.

Bob, Son of Battle didn't fill the bill, either. All I can remember about it was a lot of straining and heroism on the part of Bob: overcoming insurmountable obstacles, showing selfless loyalty, that sort of thing. I guess I wasn't sentimental enough to be deeply moved by canine heroism. I never cared all that much for dogs like Lassie. Too "uplifting." And not dog-like, not like our bird-dog Dixie, for instance. Now *that* was a dog. Scratch *Bob*.

I wouldn't have read *The Mickey Mantle Story* if Mickey Mantle hadn't been my hero. I played shortstop in little league ball; Mantle had started out as a shortstop. I was growing up in Oklahoma; Mantle had grown up there too. My dad even knew a guy up in Spavinaw who had been like an uncle to Mickey. One night, we went out to the local ballpark to watch a major league exhibition game. Mantle, after shagging a fly against the right field fence, threw a perfect bullet to home plate on the fly, and my jaw dropped. After the game, my dad's friend got us into the locker room, where we met the young "Commerce Comet," fresh from the shower and wearing nothing but a white towel and looking to me like the god Apollo himself. If all this didn't inspire me to read about his life, nothing would.

My parents must have given me *The Mickey Mantle Story*. Like a religious zealot who reads little tracts only to feed his or her fanaticism, I inhaled the book. I thought it was wonderful. In this biography, Mantle's rise to success was a foregone conclusion; therefore, everything he did was right. Also, needless to say, he led an exemplary life. He had no vices. He just played baseball and was great. Now, as an inspiration for reading other biographies, this book was a poor model. It was thoroughly ordinary. It had no grit, no particularity of character. It should have aspired to have been as good in its way as Mantle was in his, but it didn't. It was simply a commercial property about another commercial property. In other words, it was empty. Like *The Lone Ranger* and *Bob, Son of Battle,* it did not lead me to other books.

The school library didn't help, either. To me, it was just some old books on low shelves against the cafeteria walls. The librarian was a stern, tight-lipped, perpetually angry woman who trotted around the room like a doberman pinscher on the prowl, as we read silently from "the book of our choice." If she noticed anyone transgressing any of her many rules, she would slam the face of her ping-pong paddle flat against the nearest wooden table, so resoundingly that some children would actually scream. From time to time she read to us. One selection, perhaps from tales of King Arthur and the Knights of the Round Table, described a slain knight who had been placed in state and floated down-river "on a bier." I burst out laughing: the image of a dead knight floating down a river atop a glass of beer—I had never heard of a "bier"—was delightful. My misunderstanding was a consequence of trying to translate the story's antiquated diction into something I could understand. The language seemed hazy with cobwebs and dust, the language of going part-way to sleep, unable to fix on a thought or to control one's attention. This language barrier, the pre-nausea smell of the school lunch being prepared in the adjacent kitchen, the smell of spilled milk endemic to every elementary school cafeteria, the smell of musty books lining the walls, and the formidable presence of Mrs. Schultz, all combined to make the library period less than appetizing.

This tale of woe now takes an upswing, as far as reading is concerned, anyway. I went to junior high school, where I had the same English teacher for three years. One of the first things she did was give each of us a "reading wheel," a chart designed to encourage variety and balance in our choice of books. The wheel was divided into pie wedges, and at the outer edge of each was a subject heading, such as Fiction, Sports, Biography, History, or Science. Each wedge was filled with little circles. In each circle was space for a number to be keyed to a list sheet attached to the wheel. When you read a book, you wrote its title and author on the list sheet, with its numbered lines. You then wrote its number in one of the circles in the appropriate subject division on the wheel, beginning near the center of the wheel and working outward. Thus, the wheel graphically displayed one's reading patterns. If you tended to read only one type of book, the wheel looked lopsided. Our teacher encouraged us to read for pleasure, but to try to create a balanced wheel. We were required to read at least three books each semester.

The first semester, I read the minimum, or rather, less: two books about hot rods, to which I added, on the reading wheel, *The Mickey Mantle Story*. At least the hot rod books were about something that genuinely interested me. From there, over the remaining five semesters, my reading followed my interests, through astronomy and physics to literature. Even some of the assigned reading at school was interesting. This general intellectual awakening coincided with the onset of puberty and the arrival of eyeglasses, and with my increasingly playing the role of a school "brain-boy." But my English teacher played a large role in making me aware of the importance and pleasures of words. At age 13, I began writing poetry and short fiction, and sporadically keeping a journal, all for myself and, from time to time, for a few friends.

Despite the dramatic improvement, I had trouble reading in long stretches. After a while, my mind would wander or my body feel uncomfortable. I was easily distracted. My best friend, Dickie Gallup, had the same problem, and together we set out to solve it. We decided that we should first remove all the external distractions, to create what we only half ironically called a "nirvana." This meant lots of soft pillows, an oscillating fan, good lighting, soft music, a DO NOT DISTURB sign on the door, and a pitcher of some cool beverage at hand, along with a box of Lorna Doone shortbread cookies, perhaps. We also rearranged the furniture in our rooms, for optimum efficiency and as a barrier to intruders (our parents). The only problem with our nirvanas was that they were so comfortable that we fell asleep. Eventually, I dispensed with all the paraphernalia and went back to reading propped up in bed, with my knees drawn up. As long as I was locked in that position, I could keep reading. Once I stretched out my legs, though, such a soothing sensation came over me that I fell asleep immediately.

From there, through high school, I was set in my ways: I read for myself, either philosophy, because of the content, or literature, because of the style. At age 16, I devoured Jack Kerouac and Allen Ginsberg, because for me they combined the two. I got a job in a bookstore and started a small literary magazine, even publishing Kerouac, Ginsberg, and others, including myself, and I took a sacred vow, under the elms in our front yard one starry night, to be a poet. In a little over four years I had gone from being an indifferent reader to a writer, editor, and bookseller! When asked what I wanted for Christmas, I said, "A giant bookshelf."

In college, it was the same, only more so: I could pick many of my courses, and thus closely match up, for the first time, my school reading with my "outside" reading. I majored in English and comparative literature, and I was lucky to have a few extraordinary teachers. Suddenly, there was the great literature of the world spread out before me, and I read enormously, as if to make up for what I had missed as a child. I never went anywhere without a book.

In fact, after a friend and I were picked up by the Providence, Rhode Island, police on suspicion of armed robbery (we had in fact gone out for a meatball sandwich), we sat in the police station reading—he, Shakespeare's sonnets and I, a play by Shaw. The salient fact here is not that we were detained by the police, but that we both had taken books with us when we went out for a sandwich!

When most people get out of school, their reading declines or stops. The general idea is that after graduation you go out into the "real" world, for which school was the preparation. You have to get a job, earn money, raise a family, pursue a career. Unless your profession calls for it, you aren't expected to read books. You are too busy or too tired, so if you read anything, you read magazines or the newspaper. Or maybe just a menu. This diminution of reading is part of the strange idea that one's early years are for learning and the later years are for living.

Many who do continue to read limit themselves to escapist fiction or job-related nonfiction. Because I am a writer, my reading has had no such sharp distinctions between job-related or escapist. But somehow, between the ages of 23 and 43, my good reading patterns gradually eroded, so gradually that it was undetectable. Ironically, it was diminishing eyesight that made me notice this erosion.

One day I realized I couldn't make out the names in the phone book. My immediate suspicion was that the telephone company was using a smaller typeface. Some weeks later, reading the newspaper late at night, I realized that I was having more and more trouble reading moderately small type. If this continued, I wouldn't be able to read at all.

There were two results of this experience. First, I went to my optometrist, who prescribed reading glasses. Second, I started thinking about reading, which I had always taken for granted. At the moment when there arose the suggestion that at some point I might lose the ability to read, reading seemed suddenly valuable, wonderful, and even miraculous. Now I suddenly wanted to read and to know more about this ability that had become so familiar to me as to go virtually unnoticed, unappreciated, and underdeveloped.

I realized that for some time I had been unhappy with my reading. I read too sporadically, too little, and with wavering attention. What I read with greatest interest was often quirky and personal: a chainsaw manual, practical how-to books on carpentry, magic catalogues, foreign text-books, a pamphlet on Larbaud mineral water, a British magazine called *Pig Farming*, tennis magazines, issues of *House Beautiful* from the 1940s and '50s, articles on topiary gardening, and so on. I was simply following my interests, whether in the content or the style of the reading matter. I enjoyed the clarity of a few of the how-to books, and the inanity of com-mercial magazine writing. The broken English of owners' manuals from Taiwan and Hong Kong was especially delightful. My idiosyncratic read-ing reminds me of something Rimbaud wrote in *A Season in Hell*:

> I loved idiotic paintings, frieze panels, stage-sets, jugglers' backdrops, signs, popular colored prints, old-fashioned literature, Church Latin, badly-spelled pornography, the novels of our grandmothers, fairy tales, children's storybooks, old operas, silly refrains, ingenuous rhythms. (61)

My reading was light, disposable, and useful for the ways it made me read more creatively. The chainsaw manual, for instance, engaged my ability to translate written instructions into action. And since my arms and legs depended on following the instructions, I was highly attentive. I appreciated the manual's well-conceived structure, its clear and concise style, and its illustrations that matched perfectly the look of the chainsaw (I just typed "chinsaw" by mistake! Ouch!). I enjoyed translating the in-structions into real life.

The old issues of *House Beautiful*, with their marvelous, faded color photographs of interiors that existed only in the most perfect world, caused me to dream up scenarios for them, complete with charac-ters and incidents, some of them rather incongruent: through the open door that gives onto the verandah that overlooks the smooth green lawn that slopes gently down to the distant pond, I would have a gorilla enter, cross the room, sit down at the Steinway, and play the piano music of Erik Satie. The texts that accompanied the photographs evoked various imagi-nary authors for me, usually a cross between Hedda Hopper and George Sanders, whose words I would hear instead of read, as they conducted me on a guided tour of the residence. Such a Hollywood fantasy was prob-ably not unlike those my mother might have had, looking at the same is-sues when they were new.

When looking at *Pig Farming*, I'd imagine myself an English farmer, sitting in his easy chair after dinner wondering if he could improve his hus-bandry by ordering one of these newfangled castration devices. Despite the technical vocabulary, the articles were so geared to a specific audience that it became easier to imagine oneself a member of that audience.

These reading materials, as idiosyncratic as they might seem, were serving a purpose. In some oblique way, they were feeding into the poetry and fiction I was writing, by providing a sense of form and a certain remote imagery I found attractive.

But *as reading*, their value was slight. I was getting a lot of pleasure and a certain amount of instruction, but it was not edifying. Because the mental games I played with this type of reading came naturally, they presented no great challenge. I wasn't confronted with difficult material, or required to think abstractly about difficult subjects. I read virtually no metaphysics, no psychology, no philosophy. I was able to evaluate what I read, to sense its tone, to summarize its content, to criticize it, and even to parody it, only because it was lightweight material. When I realized how one-sided my reading had become and I finally returned to reading more difficult material, I saw that in some ways I had become a mental weakling. A book such as Kierkegaard's *Fear and Trembling*, which I had always wanted to read simply because of the title, was exasperatingly hard to follow at first.

I had also pretty much stopped reading fiction, especially "serious" fiction. I had never had much patience for description; I seemed to resent being told what someone or something looked like. I preferred to imagine it myself. Also, stories tended to bother me by the way they had to end; only rarely did I feel that they had a satisfying resolution, that things finally fell into place in a way that was convincing, fitting, and yet fresh. I lacked the patience to give a long, wordy novel time to get its hooks into me, so that novels such as *Vanity Fair* were out of the question.

Gradually I did more and more professional reading. Because I am a poet, a teacher of poetry writing to children, and an editor of books on creative teaching, I read a lot of contemporary poetry, book reviews, creative writing books, and general books on education, mostly to keep up with what was current, to see if anything of extraordinary interest had popped up. Not a whole lot had. The great amount of new material caused me to become more proficient at skim reading. I was reading a lot more and paying less attention to it, but worse than that was the way it narrowed my field of vision. As someone remarked, "Editors are the least well-read people I know: the only thing they read is what comes across their desks."

In short, I had become a typically educated, adult, bad reader. What I had forgotten was that the "classics," even in mediocre translation, were created by people who looked at life squarely and had something wise or beautiful to say about it, with freshness and originality. For instance, you assume that the great Montaigne's essays are going to be stuffy, high-minded, or abstract. Read his essay "On Cannibalism" and disabuse your-self. You think that Ariosto's epic poem *Orlando Furioso* is going to be too baroque and long-winded; in fact it is a wonderfully original and inventive work. The classics are never what you think they're going to be, even when you're reading them for the second time. As Maurice Blanchot says, with typically French *sérieux*,

> The book whose source is art has no guarantee in the world, and when it is read, it has never been read before; it only attains its presence as a work in the space opened by this unique reading, each time the first reading and each time the only reading. (95)

I've gone into such detail about myself as a reader because I wanted to present a model you can use in thinking about yourself as a reader. Ask yourself these questions: How does your reading history compare to mine? What are your reading attitudes and habits? Where did they come from? Are they holding you back? Are you a "passive reader"? Could you be reading better books? Could you be reading better?

3 Your Personal History

If reading is one of the most valuable things we do, then we should try to help it develop, deepen, and grow more expansive, fluid, comprehensive, and various. To do so, it helps enormously to understand what kinds of readers we are, how our reading patterns and attitudes have been formed, and what the history of our reading has been. In short, we need to know how we got to where we are, so we can see where we might go.

What follows are some basic ideas, techniques, and questions that will help you get a better idea of your history as a reader (you'll find other questions, dealing with our idiosyncracies as readers, in Chapter 5). The questions are arranged under the headings of "Before School," "At School," and "After School" because school is usually the pivotal point in our reading experience.

Before School

Try to remember what experiences you had with written words before you ever went to school.

1. Did your parents or someone else read to you or tell you bedtime stories? Did you like it? What kinds of books did they read to you? Picture books? Did you have favorites? What were they?

2. Were there favorite anecdotes that were often told at family get-togethers?

3. Were there books and magazines in your house? Who read them? Did you see your parents reading?

4. Did you play with alphabet blocks?

5. Did you go to a nursery school, a Head Start center, or a local library where stories were read aloud to you? Who read them? Did you like the stories? Did you like the reader?

6. Did you watch the reading segments on educational television shows such as *Sesame Street*? Did you enjoy them? Did you pay attention and follow the instructions?

7. What other kinds of shows did you watch? Did you watch the commercials? Which do you still remember? Do you remember any of the jingles?

8. Did you listen to stories on the radio? Were they mysteries, cowboy shows, situation comedies, or dramas?

9. Did anyone make an active, conscious effort to teach you to read? Did anyone help you read when you asked for help? If so, who? If you asked what a sign meant, did you get a positive reaction?

10. Were you taken to the library and shown how to check out books?

11. Were you given books as presents or rewards?

12. Were you encouraged to talk? Did your parents listen to you? Did they look at you when you talked to them? In your family, did one speaker often interrupt another?

13. Were you able to read? What kinds of things, and how well?

These questions are hard to answer right off the bat. For most of us, memories of our early years are locked away in distant, dusty brain cells. It takes a while to get at them. Here are some specific techniques that might help.

1. Look at photographs taken during your early years. The family album, if there is one, is a palace of windows onto the past—not only how things looked, but how they *felt*. Noticing the set of your uncle's jaw could remind you of how forbidding he seemed when you were little. Seeing a photograph of your dog can remind you what it felt like to roll around on the grass with him and have him lick your face. If you look at old photographs and sort of let yourself go, sometimes you can "fall" into them for a moment—that is, the feeling in them comes back to you.

2. Make a list, including addresses, of all the places you lived. Draw a map of the street, the area directly around the house or apartment, and a floor plan of each place. On the floor plan, mark where the doors, windows, and closets were. Include furniture and appliances, especially the television, radio, and telephone. Mark the area where your family usually put holiday decorations such as the Christmas tree or menorah. Also mark spots where books and magazines were kept: shelves, cases, tables, and racks. It helps to close your eyes and take a slow mental walk through and around the various rooms. Turn on the lights as you go.

3. Do the same for other houses you visited often, such as granny's or a neighbor's.

4. Talk to your relatives about your early years. Ask your parents or grandparents if they read to you, bought you books or magazines, or

helped you learn to read. Ask them whether or not you were curious about signs in the street and along the road. Ask them what they used to read, and what their favorite radio and television shows were.

At School

For some of us, the jump from home to school was so momentous that we are unable to recall exactly how it happened. First and second grades, when we're learning to read by school methods, are particularly hard to remember. Learning to read is so subtle and gradual that it's as if there were no starting point, as if, for instance, we've always known that *though* and *rough*, despite their similar spellings, do not rhyme. The questions below are designed to help you recall a surprising amount about how you were taught to read in school.

1. Who were the teachers who taught you to read? Did you like them? What were their names, and what did they look like? Can you remember any of their voices? What else?

2. Try to remember how they taught you. Did they use the "look–say" (word recognition) method? Did they use the phonics method? Both? Did they use what is now called a whole language approach?

3. Did your teachers read to you? At a certain grade level, did they stop reading to you? Did they ever talk about what they read at home?

4. Was there a classroom library? What was in it? Were there any books by students? Did your teacher show you how to make your own books?

5. Did you enjoy reading in school, or did you read just because it was assigned?

6. Do you recall having to read aloud in front of the class? How did you feel? Did you do well? Did it make you nervous? Proud?

7. What did the school library—or, as they're sometimes called now, the "media center"—look like? What did it smell like? Was it attractive? Why did you go there? Did you feel comfortable? Welcome? Did you check out books and read them just because you wanted to?

8. Think back to junior and senior high. Did your reading habits change? Did you have a summer vacation or a school year in which you suddenly began reading a lot more books? What books were they? Why the sudden change? Or did you read less and less?

9. How did your school reading compare with your home reading? Did your friends read? Was there peer pressure on you to read, or *not* to read? Did your social life take a lot of time away from reading?

10. Did you have reading guidance from a parent, a teacher, or a librarian, someone who made a difference?

11. Did you read books that were considered "over your head"? Or did you read books that were intended for a younger reader? Or both?

12. Did you at any point begin to find it harder to read in long stretches? Or easier?

13. Did you read books so that they would take you away from reality and into another world? Or did you read books about the everyday world?

14. Did you have favorite writers whose books you devoured? Did you have favorite books that you read over and over?

Here are some ways that might help you answer the questions above.

1. Make a list of the school(s) you attended. Draw their floor plans, as best you can. Start with the lunch room or auditorium, or any room you used year after year and therefore remember best.

2. Try to locate your school photos, the ones taken every year. If possible, arrange them in chronological order.

3. Try to locate your report cards. These are particularly valuable because they have your grades in reading and the language arts, your attendance figures, your teachers' names, your parent's signature, and sometimes what the teachers wanted your parents to know about how you were doing in school. Just holding a report card in your hand and looking at it will give you a feel for those days: the size and shape of the card, the typeface, the teacher's handwriting, all are powerful stimuli, as powerful now as they were then. If you can't find your report cards, ask the board of education for your school transcripts.

4. Try to find your school notebooks, papers, artwork, and textbooks—the older the better. In these times of increased social mobility and new houses without attics, such things tend to get thrown out. You may be surprised by what you find, though, if you scrounge around. Ask your parents and other relatives. (Mothers tend to cherish keepsakes more than fathers.) Maybe your cousins used the same textbooks as you

did. Look in the old cardboard boxes sitting up there on the garage joists. To find old textbooks, comb the used book stores, the thrift shops, and the lawn sales around where you went to school. Also, keep in mind that the same textbooks are sometimes used—and therefore can be found—in disparate parts of the country. (At a library sale in Vermont, I found the first-grade speller we had used in Oklahoma 38 years ago.) The classified ads in the *New York Times Book Review* (available at your library) usually include booksellers who will search for old books for you.

5. Visit your old school. Sit in on a class in one of your rooms. Find out if any of your teachers are still there, and if so, talk with them about how they taught reading.

6. Talk to your old classmates about your early schooling. These conversations sometimes start slowly, but they can build momentum and lead to memories that would otherwise remain inaccessible. If you're not in contact with any classmates, find out if your high school reunion committee has a current list of names and addresses; if you grew up in the same town, it's possible that some of your high school classmates also attended elementary school with you.

7. Use hypnosis as a way of "regressing" to your early days. Tell the hypnotist what you want to remember.

After School

By "after school" I mean after you got out of school "for good."

1. Did you feel that your education was complete, and so there was no need to read as much? Or was the habit of reading so rewarding and ingrained that you kept on reading at the same rate or at an increased rate?

2. Do you have friends who read, and with whom you talk about what you read?

3. Do you have bookshelves? Do they have books on them? What kinds of books? What kinds *don't* you have?

4. If you have children, did you read to them when they were little? Did you buy them books?

5. Have you ever belonged to a national or local book club? A reading group?

6. Have you ever served as a reading volunteer for a school or other organization?

7. Did you ever study speed reading? Did it make you a more versatile reader? Did it stick? Do you think it was useful?

8. Does reading seem less important, as important, or more important than it used to? How?

9. Do your eyes tire more easily than they used to? Do you use reading glasses?

10. Do you read more than one book at the same time? Do you have a tendency to abandon one book in favor of starting another, only to abandon it in turn, and so on?

11. Are there books you've always wanted to read, or told yourself you *ought* to read, but never have? Make a list of them. Do they naturally fall into certain categories? If so, do the categories tell you anything? Why do you think you've never read any of them?

12. After a hard day at work, do you find it easier to come home and watch television than to read? Or, like a jogger who needs to run every day, do you get up early so you can read for an hour each morning before you go to work?

13. Do you buy books and keep them? Do you have a particular bookshop you always look forward to? Do you underline certain passages and make marginal notes? Do you set coffee cups and drinking glasses on your books?

14. Do you use the library? Do you use it only as a last resort? Do you go there for a particular book, or to browse around and take out whatever looks appealing? Do you sometimes browse among books whose subject matter doesn't particularly interest you? Do you take care of library books as well as you take care of your own?

15. Do you read in a language other than your native language?

16. When you're alone, do you ever read aloud to yourself?

17. In response to a book, have you ever written to its author or publisher?

18. Have you ever written a book (published or unpublished)? Have you thought about writing one, or started one but never finished it?

These barrages of questions and procedures might seem overwhelming. Take them individually, allowing yourself plenty of time to mull them over. Some of them will come clear only with time. Others, whose answers seem obvious at first, become richer and more complex in light of the answers to other questions. The more you put into thinking about them, the more you will get out of them.

The purpose of the questions is to help you establish a chronology of your feelings about reading, based on the facts of your reading history. You might want to make a time line of your reading history, and add to it when you remember something new. To make a time line, get a long sheet of paper (or tape several sheets together) and turn it sideways. Draw a horizontal line across the middle. At the left, put the date of your birth. At the right, put the present date. Using answers from the questions above (and any others you might think of), fill it in with relevant dates and events in your reading history.

A good sense of yourself as a reader—how you got to where you are as a reader today—will not only make the exercises in later chapters more fruitful for you, it will also help you identify and understand any deficiencies in your reading methods, and thus give you some sense of how to develop and improve those methods.

4 Unconscious Errors in Reading

While your eyes go down the printed page, your mind will be going between the lines, in and out and under and beyond the words.

—John Waldman

My recollections of being taught to read in school are echoed by Bruno Bettelheim and Karen Zelan in their book, *On Learning to Read: The Child's Fascination with Meaning*. These authors believe that children are alienated from reading because the basal readers used in school are dull, pointless, vacuous, and therefore patronizing, and that a child's (oral, and perhaps silent) reading mistakes are often an unconscious reaction to the tedium of the material in general or to a particular word that is too emotionally charged to be read correctly. Bettelheim and Zelan urge textbook authors and publishers to make preprimers and primers more commensurate with the intelligence of students; they urge educators not to see children's reading mistakes simply as errors in decoding (the use of phonics), but to understand the psychological significance of such errors.

Of particular interest to Bettelheim, whose background is in psychoanalysis, is the role of the unconscious in reading:

> A vast literature is devoted to the problem of how a writer's or an artist's unconscious influences his work. Equally as important is the share the unconscious plays in shaping the *reader's* appreciation of a work of literature. The unconscious of the reader significantly shapes his responses to the work he is reading, but so far this phenomenon has received little attention, although its investigation would help us to understand why some people derive great benefit from reading while others remain indifferent to it.

> Any piece of writing contains overt and covert messages. The person who is reading it responds to both types of messages with both conscious and unconscious reactions. In consequence, the meanings intended by an author and those which the reader derives from what the author has written are by no means identical. (40)

This last point is particularly true of writing—such as modern poetry—that is by nature allusive or suggestive, rather than explicit or strictly informative. It is also true of writing from distant cultures and ancient times, wherein the original context is so fragmentary that we can only guess at what it all means. So, in these cases, we rely on our intuition to a greater degree than normal. We allow our unconscious selves to take a larger part in the reading.

The mainstream, traditional attitude implies that readers should try to derive from a piece of writing exactly what the author intended to communicate. Such a task is unrealistic because it is impossible. In the first place, the author doesn't always know exactly what he or she intended to communicate. Much printed material is filled with hazy phrases, thoughtless clichés, and dubious word choices that belie the author's inability to write or think precisely. Some authors *sort of* know what they intended, and the result is *more or less* clear writing. In the second place, authors sometimes are unaware that their motives may be other than they think; unconscious motives or moments have a way of insinuating themselves into the fiber of the work. (As one of John Ashbery's poems says, "He'd tell 'em by their syntax.") How is the reader to know if what was intended was the same as what was expressed? College literature classes are filled with students, some of them quite bright, who analyze a work of literature on the basis of intentions they ascribe to the author, and then measure the work against those presumed intentions. Quite often the author is then faulted for not doing or doing poorly what he or she never intended to do. As Aristotle put it:

> We should think how best we shall avoid the fault described by Glaucon when he says that critics make unreasonable presuppositions, and go on to draw conclusions from their own adverse comments on the poet; if his words conflict with the conclusions they have thus reached, they censure him as though he had actually said what they ascribe to him. (72-73)

Even trying to evaluate authors' stated intentions is tricky business; sometimes there's a big difference between what authors intended and what they *say* they intended.

Of course, there are simpler cases in which the author's intention is clear. If an author writes "The doctor looked down her throat," we are startled to hear a student read it aloud as "The doctor looked down the road." In terms of decoding, the disparity between intention and interpretation is blatant. Such an error might well be caused by an unconscious reaction on the child's part. Bettelheim and Zelan remind us that children are more susceptible than adults to having their emotions affect their perceptions; they are more subjective, less able to prevent the unconscious from "distorting" more objective versions of reality. (A positive way of stating this is to say that children are in closer touch with their imaginations.) The child, by modifying what he or she is reading, "actively masters in personal ways that which otherwise he would only passively be taking in" (Bettelheim and Zelan 42). (I should interject here that the more sophisticated view of reading as transactional, in which the reader actively participates in creating the meaning of the text, rejects any notion of passivity in reading.)

Bettelheim and Zelan go on to say that "whether a child will develop a deep and lasting commitment to reading will be strongly influenced by whether he views reading as something imposed on him from the outside, or as something in the creation of which he actually participates" (43).

Bettelheim and Zelan are not claiming that unconscious mistakes ("modifying") in reading make children better readers, only that we ought to understand the role of unconscious mistakes so they can be overcome. In *On Learning to Read*, many of the examples follow the same pattern: the child misreads a word, the observer (Bettelheim or a colleague) calls attention to the misreading in a neutral or positive way, the child acknowledges the mistake and sometimes realizes what personal experience ultimately contributed to the mistake, and then, having brought this unconscious feeling to light, goes on to read the word correctly. This procedure sounds a bit too tidy, but it has its uses.

It would be nice if all teachers were sensitive to such a technique; it would be nice if, being so sensitive, they had the time to devote this much attention to each student. The way things are, perhaps the best one can hope for now is that all reading teachers be made aware that "miscues" in reading are not always caused by disabilities or poor decoding skills. In fact, according to Ken Goodman, good readers make some types of miscues more often than poor readers, but miscues that are harmless, such as those involving function words and pronouns (Weaver 126).

Bettelheim and Zelan see a hidden bonus in unconscious errors:

> It is a strange fact that in our teaching of reading to beginners we neglect their active manipulation of reading [their meaningful mistakes], which would and could make it a significant personal experience for them. We involve only the child's intellect in the process of learning to read, and we exclude his unconscious life from participating in it. (43)

In terms of the present work, I would change "unconscious" to "creative." Freudians (such as Bettelheim and Zelan) value the unconscious, poets (such as myself) value the creative. And there is a difference. It is one thing to have a nightmare, it is another to write like Kafka. So when Bettelheim and Zelan recommend that we involve the child's "total personality in the process of reading," I would argue that such an involvement, as desirable as it is, is in fact only partial. It is not artistic. It does not encourage the child (or adult) to become a really active reader, a reader who feels free to rearrange, reinterpret, rebuild the text, following his or her most subjective or imaginative or whimsical impulse.

This artistic, active, "aggressive" (root meaning: to go toward) attitude can help prepare the reader to meet head-on the swelling wave of poorly written books, newspapers, magazines, film and television scripts, newsletters, memoranda, and other materials that issue forth from a country whose verbal ability seems to have declined—if we are to believe the sinking numbers scored by students on national reading and writing tests, or if we are to believe college teachers who say that today's students are far less literate than those of, say, 30 years ago. You can blame it all on television, on drugs, on rock 'n' roll, on the family (or lack of it), on the schools, or on anything else you choose, but it will not alter the fact that an increasing amount of what is published these days is so slipshod or vacuous that, in self-defense, you will have to change it or half ignore it as you read, just so you can get to the parts that have that little something you were looking for. You have to be more aggressive in reading bad or mediocre books, or they will flatten you out and roll right over you with their relentless momentum.

Take the mediocre mystery novel. John Waldman, a speed-reading specialist, told me that when he was a soldier, in the Second World War, he passed the slack time reading mystery novels, no matter how trashy, but the first time through he read only the odd-numbered pages, the second time through, a few weeks later, only the even-numbered. He did so merely to break his habit of feeling he had to read every word of every page in a book, but a side-effect was that the stories became more challenging and interesting: he had to help fill in the missing parts. This procedure engaged him creatively in the reading; and in effect, he got two books for the price of one.

John was intentionally misreading those mystery novels. He was cultivating the creative use of what would ordinarily be considered a mistake. But what about reading mistakes that are neither intentional (like Waldman's) nor unconscious (like those described by Bettelheim and Zelan)? Some of these other—and much more common—reading mistakes are discussed in the next chapter.

5 Two Normal Eyes and Nine Everyday Mistakes

Jumping across, eyes read a book.
—Edwin Denby

At this very moment, your eyes are doing something strange and wonderful. They are skipping along these black marks and sending signals to your brain, where something even stranger and more wonderful is happening. You are reading.

This is obvious. But the *way* you do it is not obvious at all. Nor is the way you *don't* do it. You read well or you read poorly, or you read some things well and others poorly, or you read well sometimes and poorly at others. All this you know, more or less consciously, from having gone to school, where you were tested, tested, tested, and where you got a sense of your reading ability.

But what is reading ability? In the traditional definition, it is a combination of comprehension and speed: the more you understand of what you read, and the quicker you do it, the better you are at it. Comprehension means more than just being able to say what each individual word means, or each individual phrase, or each individual sentence. Comprehension includes being able to sense nuance, changes of tone, and the author's "voice"; to make reasonable assumptions about what the author might mean but does not say explicitly; and to relate what you read to what you know. Speed means more than velocity. It also encompasses fluidity and ease, which enable the reader to read quickly for extended periods, without tiring. It also means knowing when to skip or skim over those parts of a text that are not relevant to your purposes. Imparting comprehension and speed is the goal of the traditional reading teacher.

In working toward comprehension and speed, however, we readers make mistakes. Among these are the ones I'll call *visual* (specialists include them under the broad heading of "the psychology of reading"). To understand those visual mistakes, we have to go back to the fundamentals of the act of reading: eyeball on page of type.

In reading English, we usually follow our written symbols in a particular sequence: we go from left to right on each line, from the top to the bottom of each page, and from front to back in each book. Other languages are read in other directions—Chinese (classically top to bottom) and Hebrew (right to left), for instance. Sometimes English is read otherwise, as in vertical signs. Using sophisticated methods, reading specialists discovered that the eye gazes on a group of letters in a line, takes them in, and then jumps to the next group of letters. Each time the eye stops and gazes is called a *fixation*. A jump between fixations is called a *saccade* (from a French word meaning a start, jerk, or jolt). At the end of each line, the eye *sweeps* back to the beginning of the next line.[1] When the eye stops and goes back to reread something, it is called a *regression*. Better readers take in more characters per fixation, spend less time doing it, and have fewer regressions. According to researchers, average twelfth graders spend one-quarter of a second on each fixation, during which they take in 1.3 words, for a reading rate of 250 words per minute (Taylor et al.). Specialists have devised any number of ingenious experiments to discover what happens when our eyes read, but it all boils down to the fact that our reading is parcelled out in horizontal bar-shapes:

It's almost as if we're looking at the page through slits.

It can be argued that not everyone follows this pattern: the Chinese do not have one eye directly above the other. Still, most of us who were brought up reading English (and other languages with similar directional patterns) habitually perceive words in these horizontal bar-shapes. It's possible that this structure of seeing affects the way we "read" other things—streets, landscapes, and art. This is a thorny subject that branches off into other disciplines. In any case, my opthalmologist tells me our eyes do function better moving side to side than they do moving up and down.

Advertisers know this.

F
a
r
m
e
r

is harder to read than

farmer

and

r
e
m
r
a
f

is harder still. Advertisers, who need to lock into our ingrained habits as quickly and surely as possible, stick pretty much to the horizontal bar-shape.

Our eyes do a different kind of reading when looking at works of art. There is no one way to "read" a painting, though the painting sug-gests—through its lines, masses, tones, and spatial relationships—a way or ways of reading it. If we just relax and gaze upon a painting, the paint-ing will often "tell" our eyes where to go and at what pace. (See Figure 8.) Seen thus, no two paintings will be read following the same pattern. Moreover, on subsequent viewings, the eye will find a different starting point, so that the painting will not be read the same way as the first time. There are any number of equally good starting points in a painting,

Figure 8. "Reading" a painting.

which is one of the reasons art stays fresh: the same piece never looks quite the same.

Gertrude Stein said something similar about writing: you *can't* say the same thing twice. The second time it sounds different precisely because it is the second time. The echoes of sound and sense change the *feel* of the thing said. For example, read every word in the following poem silently:

> Nothing in that drawer.
> Nothing in that drawer.
> Nothing in that drawer.
> Nothing in that drawer.
> Nothing in that drawer.
> Nothing in that drawer.
> Nothing in that drawer.
> Nothing in that drawer.
> Nothing in that drawer.
> Nothing in that drawer.
> Nothing in that drawer.
> Nothing in that drawer.
> Nothing in that drawer.
> Nothing in that drawer.

(Padgett, *Great Balls of Fire 3*)

Did every *nothing* feel the same? Every *in, that,* and *drawer*? Is the tone of each line exactly the same as that of every other line? It can't be.

Now read the poem *aloud*, and ask yourself the same questions. The difference will be more obvious. For me there are more noticeable tonal changes in two of the four words: *nothing* jumps out in certain lines, *that* is more heavily emphasized in others. In addition, from start to finish, there is a tonal curve. For me, the poem begins in a quiet, normal manner, the way a casual search does, but by line 6 the tone becomes a little irritated and even frenetic from this fruitless search; by line 10 it has become exasperated; by line 12 the pace slows, with a sense of resignation that gradually slows us toward the final line, where the tone of closure seems to say "well, that's that, there's no more I can do." For you, the poem may have a different set of tones—another example of the idea that you can't say the same thing twice.

Another way to sense the impossibility of a perfectly uniform repetition is to do what you probably did as a child: repeat any word over and over and over and over. Pick a work, any word. Now say it aloud for five minutes. Actually do this now.

Did you cheat and keep reading? If so, you are as contrary as I am. And you will have missed something. You will have missed the disorienting experience of seeing a word gradually drained of its meaning, reduced to its acoustical properties, to abstraction, to virtual nonsense. What may have started out as the name of your beloved might well have ended up as gibberish—a transformation from the most meaningful to the least. And yet, through all these changes, it was the "same" word.

You will also have missed noticing how your attention varied. It might have been fixed first on repeating the word at regular intervals; then on how the word sounded; then how your tongue, teeth, and lips were moving to form its various parts; then on how nutty the exercise seems; then suddenly back on the word as a signifier of something out there in the real world, with rain water dripping from its leaves and branches, and so on.

So, if you cheated, go back now and repeat aloud the same word for five minutes.

The point of all this is that the perceiving mind is constantly shifting and wavering, like a distant radio station.[2] Our perceptual power fades in and out: we simply cannot bring a perfectly steady attention to bear on each and every word, sentence, and paragraph, page after page. Even if we could, the words themselves would not be equally engaging. Sometimes, through no fault of our eye or mind, we find ourselves reading the wrong word. There is a whole group of reading errors that have little or nothing to do either with errors in decoding or with emotional disruption: in other words, errors that are not wholly due to a simple inability to read or a bugaboo in the unconscious.

Few people talk about these glitches in so-called normal reading, and yet such glitches happen frequently. See if you've experienced any of the nine mistakes listed below.

1. *The single word error*. Poet Paul Hoover has written, "Whenever I see New Haven, I often say/New Heaven" (55). The price sticker covers the *s* on my can of shaving soap, so it reads: "New Noxema / have / Heavy Beard." The neon sign at the corner is half burned out, changing *Victor's Meat Market* into *Victor's Me*. The word *olfactory* breaks into two parts, creating an image of closed steel mills or auto plants. The weatherman makes a droll report: "Outside the humility is at 43 percent."

As an adolescent, I consistently misread "realty" as "reality." I was entering puberty and, appropriately enough, had just learned the word *reality*. I was fascinated that there even could be such a thing as reality. It had never occurred to me. Suddenly, all over town, I noticed little signs advertising Farmer Reality, Mudd Reality, Home Reality, Admiral Reality, and so on. Of course I knew that there was no such thing as a reality company, and I knew that there was another word there, but it gave me great delight nonetheless to transform, for a moment, these commonplace signs into symbols of phenomenology.

It reminds me of how my grandfather used his failing hearing: he heard pretty much what he wanted to hear. Sometimes he pretended not to have heard at all. Other times, he'd repeat, in slightly different words, what had just been said to him. If my grandmother would say, "Noah, go to the store and buy a gallon of milk," he might answer, "You want me to buy a gal some milk?" His mishearing was vaguely intentional, but perhaps not to the extent that he was always aware of its being so. I've known other elderly people who heard selectively, but not many who replied with such deadpan distortions of what they'd just heard. This type of character is more often seen in movie comedies made in the 1930s and 1940s, when the comedy of errors blossomed in so many forms, including the misheard one-liner.

The British novelist Henry Green also seems to have had a penchant for mishearing, as in his *Paris Review* interview:[3]

> *Interviewer:* I've heard it remarked that your work is "too sophisticated" for American readers, in that it offers no scenes of violence—and "too subtle," in that its message is somewhat veiled. What do you say?
>
> *Mr. Green:* Unlike the wilds of Texas, there is very little violence over here. A bit of child-killing of course, but no straight shootin'. After fifty, one ceases to digest; as someone once said: "I just ferment my food now." Most of us walk crabwise to meals and everything else. The oblique approach in middle-age is the safest thing. The unusual at this period is to get anywhere at all—God damn!
>
> *Interviewer:* And how about "subtle"?
>
> *Mr. Green:* I don't follow. *Suttee,* as I understand it, is the suicide—now forbidden—of a Hindu wife on her husband's flaming bier. I don't want my wife to do that when my time comes—and with great respect, as I know her, she won't. . . .
>
> *Interviewer:* I'm sorry, you misheard me; I said, "subtle"—that the message was too subtle.
>
> *Mr. Green:* Oh, *subtle.* How dull!

(Green 64–65)

I suspect that Green, who earlier in the interview had claimed to be "a trifle hard of hearing," used his disability selectively, in this case as a "veiled" response to a "dull" question (Kermode 13).

Freud discusses misreading and its oral equivalent, the slip of the tongue, in his essay, "Psychopathology of Everyday Life":

> Both irritating and laughable is a lapse in reading to which I am frequently subject when I walk through the streets of a strange city during my vacation. I then read *antiquities* on every shop sign that shows the slightest resemblance to the word. . . ." (88)

Later in the same essay he claims, somewhat broadly, that "back of every error is a repression" (142).

Not all of my reading "mistakes" (such as "reality" for "realty") are the result of unconscious repression. Like those of Henry Green and my grandfather, they are a mechanism of evasion, but they are semi-conscious. Recently I let myself go, reading a *New York Times* article about the universe:

> One of these problems arose from the fact that the observable universe is remarkably smooth; it looks essentially the same in all directions and from all directions. Another problem is that the universe seems to contain just about the right density of matter to exert the gravity needed to slow the universal expansion and bring it to an eventual halt. The possibility that random chance alone could account for this precise density of matter strikes many cosmetologists as extremely unlikely. (April 14, 1987, p. C4)

A slip of the eye turned cosmologists into beauticians.

2. *Jumping a line*. Sometimes in sweeping back to the left-hand margin of a text, I inadvertently skip a line. This is particularly true when two consecutive lines begin with the same word or string of words. When two consecutive lines begin with the same words as they just did, the eyes are like the drunk who staggers down his street, which is lined with identical homes. If he chooses the wrong one, funny things can happen. But even funnier things happen when the eyes skip one line and continue with another that makes a perfect grammatical blend. Here's an example (without, however, the duplicate words at the beginning of each line):

> In the wild 1927 season, the great Babe Ruth hit 60
> home runs. It made him a national hero, an odd idol for
> women. Which is odd, because normally he wasn't the. . . .

If your sweep left jumps from line 1 to line 3, "women" becomes the object of the verb "hit," creating an image of Babe Ruth not as a batter but as a batterer.

These are special instances. Generally, line jumping doesn't seem to have these psychological provocations. It happens more often when the lines are too long, or when we're too tired or harried to concentrate.

3. *Looping a line*. This is another wrong line-number routine. Instead of jumping from line 1 to line 3, the eye sweeps from the end of line 1 to what should be line 2, but is in fact back at line 1 again. Example:

> I was walking down the street, daydreaming that
> you were there with me, that it was the start. . . .

Line 1, accidentally read twice, begins to form a series of Chinese boxes, mirrors reflecting mirrors, a sort of *déjà lu*. Such looping seems to occur more often when the line spacing is tight (when there isn't much white space between the lines) or when the lines are quite long.

4. *Transposing up*. In transposing up, we take a word from the next line and bring it up into the line we're reading. This happens more often when the word transposed up resembles one in the line above it, as in

> He is a man who acts in good conscience and
> whose perspicacity makes him conscious of
> those perceptions that are sometimes erroneous.

There are two main transposition trouble spots in this example: it's easy for the eye to replace *conscience* with *conscious* and *perspicacity* with *perceptions*. This is because the eye, although fixated on a single line, takes in much more, in its peripheral vision.

Certain words "catch" our eye, causing us to jump lines. The adolescent eye will pick up words such as *sex* several lines ahead of time. Our own names seem to jump out at us, as shown in Freud's quotation of the German psychologist Bleuler:

> While reading, I once had the intellectual feeling of seeing my name two lines below. To my astonishment, I found only the words *blood corpuscles*. Of the many thousands of lapses in reading in the peripheral as well as in the central field of vision that I have analyzed, this was the most striking case. Whenever I imagined that I saw my name, the word that induced this illusion usually showed a greater resemblance to my name than the words *blood corpuscles*. In most cases, all the letters of my name had to be close together before I could commit such an error. (142)

The power of one's own name, of course, is extraordinary. How many times have you heard your name called, only to turn and find that someone had said something else? How is it that we can sleep soundly while another person's name is spoken, but wake right up when our own is pronounced?

There is another, non-psychological reason for transposing up: anticipation. Anticipation is essential for good reading.[4] Poor readers go from word to word, as if stepping across a stream, pausing at each and every rock. Good readers are able to "see" ahead to get a pretty good idea of what's coming, in essence, to be able to step on only the best rocks for a smooth crossing. Anticipation comes with more experience with language. I know that *nine* is going to come at the end of "A stitch in time saves. . . ." A second grader who can read all the words in that proverb, but who has never heard it, would not of course be able to anticipate the final word. The greater our sophistication, the further our anticipation extends, and the further it extends, the hazier it becomes, and the more likely we are to make mistakes up ahead.

Good readers don't have to focus on every word: they "know" some words by their shapes, their positions in particular sentences, and by the probability of their being there. For instance, good readers read the word *the* without paying much attention to it. You paid less attention to the first occurrence of *the* in the previous sentence than you did to the second, partly because the latter was italicized, partly because it is unusual to see *the* in front of a preposition—"the word" is a much more common pattern than "the without." Good readers quickly recognize usual word patterns because they anticipate them, both visually and contextually. By that I mean that a good reader sees them out of the corner of his or her eye *and* out of the corner of his or her mind. For example, take the following sentence:

I am proud to be a citizen of the United States.

It can be read in what seems to be one smooth gulp, because it consists of simple words in predictable patterns and it expresses a commonplace sentiment. When altered, it reads less easily—and more interestingly:

I am proud to be a denizen of the United States. (One word change. *Denizen* isn't the kind of word you'd expect in such a sentence.)

I am proud to be the citizen of a United States. (Transposition of the articles *a* and *the*.)

I am united to be a state of the proud citizen. (Transposition of nouns and adjectives. In making *States* singular and lower case, I cheated a little.)

I am to be the United States. (Removal of words turns the sentence into an utterance by Walt Whitman or a contemporary would-be Louis "L'état, c'est moi" XIV.)

I am of the states united to be a proud citizen. (Multiple transpositions causes the sentence to sound like those spoken by members of Congress, when the unnatural formality of their public discourse causes them to misplace their prepositional phrases.)

States united the of citizen a be to proud am I. (Reversal of word order.)

Notice that even in the previous example you might feel little movements toward normal syntax and meaning, as if there might be some kind of person classified as an "of citizen"; as if the words *a* and *to* are typographical errors for *and* and *too*; as if the sentence were being said in dialect, perhaps by someone who had become an "of" citizen: States united the "of" citizen and be too proud, am I.

The least readable permutation avoids the usual syntactical patterns, as in:

Citizen the a states to proud I united am be of.

Interestingly, this permutation was the most difficult for me to come up with. Good readers are so locked into formal patterns that they find it hard and even nerve-wracking to try to function outside of such patterns. The patterns provide an order to our reading, one that parallels the order we sense simply in knowing who we are. These and other patterns in our lives are so strong that they enable us to continue functioning smoothly when parts of the patterns are missing. Look at the following example.

Today was Betty's sixteenth birth____, so she felt she had the right to take a little nap before din____. Then the ph____ started ringing. She knew her m____r was in the kitchen, her hands sticky from kneading the bread dough, so she hopped out of b____ and hurried down the s____s. Betty picked up the receiver and said, "H____, this is B____ speaking.

It was her f____. "Oh, hi, ____," she said. "Where are ____? It's 5:30."

"I'm still at the _____," he complained. "I thought I'd be home by now," he continued, "but the way things are _____, I don't think I'll get out of here for another ____ or so. You and _____ can go ahead and have _____ without me."

So far, you probably haven't had much trouble filling in the blanks with reasonable possibilities. The syntax and context are conventional, and the words omitted are far fewer than those given. (In *Reading without Nonsense,* Frank Smith says that "texts that are comprehensible in the first place—that are not nonsense—remain comprehensible even if up to one word in five is completely obliterated" [62].) See what happens now when more words are omitted and the story takes a surreal turn:

> At that moment the house started to _____, and Betty flew into a tree, where the amazing _____ had _____ started to _____ under _____. And Betty's _____ ____ to Pennsylvania. Dante _____ looking _____ without _____ cucumber.

Even more pernicious (or challenging, depending on your point of view) is material such as the following:

> Santa Claus was dressed in his usual red b_____ and sported his traditional white z_____, around which were assembled the b_____s that pulled his d_____ through the sky.

In this example, the hints confound rather than help us, because they take advantage of our expectations. What article of clothing starts with *b*, is red, and is normally worn by Santa? Not his belt, which is black. Not a bowtie, babuska, bandolier, bikini, or Borsalino. Even worse is his "traditional white z_____." A zither? Certainly not a Zulu. The text becomes rather fantastical and poetic if we insert *beehive, zephyr*, *bananas*, and *devastation* into the slots.

5. *Edge blur*. My eyes tend to misread the words near the beginnings and ends of the lines. I misread words at the end of the line because, being a heavy anticipator, I sweep too early. I miss words at the start of the line because I'm too hasty about recovering from the sweep and getting on with it, trying too hard to sustain my forward momentum. In both cases the fixation is rushed. Thus, the nearer to the center of the line a word is, the more likely I am to read it correctly. All the above applies equally to the whole page: I foul up more often with the first and last few words.

6. *Page skips*. Page skipping is caused by turning two or more leaves instead of one. Imagine an open book, with page 37 on the right-hand side (as it always is, being an odd-numbered page). Normally, after finishing page 37, you'd turn the leaf over to page 38 (on the left side of the next two-page spread). But if you turn two leaves, page 40 is on the left. As in jumping a line (#2 above), the result can be interesting, especially when there is a perfect grammatical dovetail between the end of one page and the beginning of the next. Even when the fit is poor, its very incongruity can be tonic, due to the sudden switch from ordinary, proper syntax to a jagged, nonsyntactical leap. Sometimes I'm shocked by how long it takes me to realize that such a leap has taken place; I'll be three or four lines down the page before a little bell goes off in my head to remind me that something wasn't quite right, up there at the start of the page.

7. *Page repeats* are the opposite of page skips. Repeats usually happen only when we return to a book after being away from the page

for a long while. The longer we're away from it, the less well we remember it, and hence we're more likely to reread it without realizing we're doing so. There are those moments, though, when we close a book for an hour, pick it up, and read deep into a passage, until it dawns on us that this is the same part we read only an hour ago. We're embarrassed, but relieved that there were no witnesses.

8. *Eye–mind split*. The eye can recognize words—and we can pronounce them correctly—without our having any idea of what they mean. Normally our attention is sustained by meaning. What happens to the mind during those moments when it "reads" but doesn't understand a word or phrase? Sometimes it makes inferences from the context. Sometimes it goes blank. Sometimes it fills in with a standard I-ought-to-look-that-up-someday reaction, then goes on. Whatever it does, it momentarily splits away from the meaning of the word or phrase.

For example, I used to have trouble with the word *atavism*. I could never remember what it meant, no matter how often I looked it up, and its context never seemed to provide a sufficient clue as to its meaning. I didn't know its root meaning, and I was never able to come up with the right mnemonic device for it.

Instead, as soon as my eye hit the word, I froze. Then I would tell myself to relax and just let my mind go: surely the meaning will come to me. I began to free-associate. In my mind's eye, I would see a large jungle clearing at night, with a group of primitive people hopping up and down in front of a bonfire dedicated to the carved image of their deity, a totem pole with pointed head and almond eyes curling upwards at the outer points. The muffled, guttural growl of their tribal chant was reverberating out into the darkness around them. Their blood sacrifice was being delayed because they had no victim, *yet*. I panicked: would they see me?

I opened my eyes. In my hands, I was still holding the book. I reread the sentence in question, projecting my fantasy onto the word *atavistic*. It didn't quite fit, so I consulted the dictionary and then reread the sentence, which made perfect sense. But within 10 minutes *atavism* began to fade again. After many years of this, I finally wrote about it, and as soon as I did, the problem vanished.

Eye-mind split also happens to good readers who have good vocabularies and who are reading perfectly understandable material: the eyes move along the words, but the mind is elsewhere.

It happens when we write, too, because the fingers are slower than the mind. The mind doesn't like to wait around too much, so it fills in the slack periods with miscellaneous material, from fleeting images to full-blown fantasies. For example, two sentences above, when I was writing "the mind is somewhere else," *my* mind was somewhere else, remembering the time that my tennis partner played an unusually poor game and explained his lack of concentration with "I was on a beach in Florida." When absorbed in reading, we listen single-mindedly to the words of the author, as if no other external stimuli were affecting us. The truth is, though, that we can't maintain such constant absorption indefinitely. Our attention wavers in and out, sometimes so far out that our eyes keep moving over the words while our minds are a few inches (or a million miles) away. This fluctuation seems normal to me. I wonder why teachers don't mention it. It would help students become aware of when their minds have wandered too far, and enable them to "return" to the text, again and again if need be.

If the mind wanders because of some uncontrollable external stimulus—the neighbor's stereo is blasting, the smell of popcorn is wafting in from the kitchen, or the heat and humidity are oppressive—it takes an effort of will to block it out. In those cases when you can't block out the distraction, no matter how hard you try, it's best to close the book and rest a moment. Or buy your neighbor some earphones, or dash into the kitchen to claim your share of the popcorn, or take a cold shower.

Mindfulness can be developed. The anxious tennis player who takes his or her eyes off the ball can repeat "ball, ball, ball, ball" all the way through a couple of points to reestablish an unbroken contact between eyes and ball. The meditating Buddhist has to be sensitive to when the beautifully empty mind has wandered onto a subject or fantasy, so that it can be called back to the desired emptiness. When I can't fall asleep quickly, I use my own version of counting sheep. I call up a visual image of a white lawn chair, and I mentally examine its parts from various angles, being careful to exclude other objects—and particularly people—from the scene. If people do enter, I stop the fantasy and start over with the white chair, no matter how many times it takes. The more I've practiced this procedure, the more effective it's become. I'm usually fast asleep within a few minutes. The more we detect the eye–mind split in reading, the more we can redirect our attention to what we read.

9. *Column confusion*. Magazines and newspapers are produced in multiple columns. This format gives them greater flexibility than that of the usual book page, which is, in effect, printed in a single column (or block) of type. Magazines and newspapers are often produced in great haste, with last-minute editorial revisions, on-the-spot solutions to graphic problems, and mounting deadline hysteria. This haste can result in the columns of type being laid out in a pattern confusing to the reader, partic-

ularly when the bottom of the column of a magazine article on plumbing says "Continued on p. 69," and when you continue on page 69 it's about eye shadow. I happen to enjoy these confusions. It's refreshing to the mind to experience such surprises and leaps. Sometimes I've gone on to the next column, discovered it's the wrong one, but continued to read it because it turned out to be more interesting than the one I was reading.

Let's face it, by the time you have to turn to page 69, the article has probably shot its bolt anyway. The fact that the typeface on page 69 is smaller tells you something, as does the fact that the words are now surrounded by small, black-and-white advertisements. How can you read about saving your soul when the little box next to the words urges you to earn big money at home in your spare time by stuffing envelopes?

Actually, I like these little ads. The older the magazine is, the more interesting they are—unlike the feature articles, which tend to age badly. But now I've gotten off the subject—appropriately enough, since it was about getting shunted into the wrong column.

———

All nine of these reading errors can be minimized by practicing mindfulness: gently but firmly drawing one's attention back to the material at hand. But if you want to go further, to learn to use these errors creatively, Chapter 6 is for you.

6 Creative Reading Techniques

One must be an inventor to read well....Then there is creative reading as well as creative writing.

—Emerson

Reading creatively involves an aggressive attitude toward the material at hand: the book is there for you to use as you see fit. It may have content that you want to extract, it may be in a writing style you want to learn, it may lend itself to self-parody, or it may invite radical revision, rearrangement, or complete transformation. In all these cases, the book is raw material for you to shape. When you come to it ready to take it apart and put it back together, it has lost its inviolability, its implied claim to immutability, its intimidating authority. You become the new author. You assume *authority*.

The first time you underline a passage or make a marginal note, you take a first step toward getting on top of the material. You begin to cast off the restriction, placed on us at an early age, against "defacing" books. As children, we are not supposed to "mess up" books, especially school readers, in which our names are inscribed at the start of the year, along with a description of the book's condition, for which we are responsible. The ostensible reason for keeping a book clean is that it's thrifty: the school needs that copy for students in subsequent years. Besides, it's worthwhile to teach children how to take care of objects. Fine and good. When it comes to books, though, such a taboo has the effect of reinforcing the power of the printed word. We are forbidden to deface the sacred tablets.

In college, though, where we are required to own our textbooks, underlining is encouraged, as an aid to study. Underlining is, in effect, a form of notetaking; instead of copying out a long passage into our notebooks, we simply underline it in pencil or ink, or lay a thick band of transparent ink over it with a fat Magic Marker. Our marginal notes tell us what we felt to be important in the material, and why. And if, at the end of the course, we sell the book back to the college bookstore, we see it join large stacks of the same title, all underlined, notated, and personalized. Seen simply as physical object, the book has lost its inviolability.

Of course, serious students know that what is important is not necessarily the physical object, but the information and sometimes the wisdom it imparts. Serious students will consume a good book the way they wolf down a great dinner. If, in the process, the book becomes marked up and unfit for anyone else, it is due not to negligence or vandalism, but to the nourishing of the mind and spirit. Marking up a book is also a step in the direction of creative reading.

But it's surprising how many young people never learn that books can be read in many different ways, depending on one's purpose. They pick up a book, read the title page, the table of contents, the acknowledgements, the foreword, the preface, the introduction, and only then begin the trek from chapter to chapter, reading every word along the way. And when they get to the end, they read (or at least look at) the bibliography and index. Their intentions are good but their method is rigid. This is similar to the attitude of the infant who demands that every word of his or her favorite bedtime story be read in exactly the same order every time.

More sophisticated students know how to get from a book what they need. They learn this from a teacher, from a course or book on how to study, or from their own experience. It is tremendously liberating to learn that you don't *have* to read a book from cover to cover. So, in reading for information, it is much more efficient to take the following steps:

1. Ask yourself what you need from the book.

2. To sense whether or not the book will give you what you need, think for a moment about its title and subtitle.

3. Carefully read the table of contents. A good table of contents gives you an outline or brief overview of the book.

4. Scan the preface or introduction. Often these will tell you why the author wrote the book and what its general message is.

5. Scan the index. A good index can give you an immediate and more specific sense of the book's contents.

6. Turn through the book, chapter by chapter, scanning the first and last few paragraphs of each. You might also read the first and last sentences in some of the paragraphs that catch your eye.

7. Go back and read the table of contents again. By now it will make more sense to you, and you should be able to add a little meat to its skeleton. Going back to the table of contents helps tie it all together.

8. Finally, ask yourself these questions: Does the book seem to have in it what you need? Is it pleasant to look at and hold? Does the type look nice, or at least unobtrusive? When necessary, does it have suitable and interesting illustrations? Is the author's style clear? Do you have a gut feeling you're going to like this book?

If the answers are all yes, eureka, you've discovered the right book for you at that moment. If the answers are mostly no, then look elsewhere, or, if it's assigned reading, read it with the foreknowledge that you probably won't enjoy it as much as you might have. It's a great advantage to understand this in advance—otherwise, your irritation can get in the way of learning whatever it is you have to learn from the book.

This preliminary scanning takes only a few minutes, but saves you a lot of grief and misery. It will help you figure out which parts are more relevant and valuable for your course of study, enabling you to skim or skip parts that are of little or no use to you.

Reading tips such as the above have been repeated—if not always heeded—for generations. It was always understood that this method applies to textbooks, nonfiction, and the like; it was an aid to study. No one has suggested that other types of material be read in a similar fashion. No one has suggested that we read only the first and last lines of each poem in a collection of poetry, or the first and last paragraphs of each chapter of a novel. Poetry and fiction are Art, which is not to be tampered with. Oh?

The exercises that follow offer some ways to read *anything* creatively. Some are more radical than others, but underlying them all are four beliefs:

1. We perceive something better by knowing what it isn't. (Sometimes when you aren't quite sure how to spell a word, don't you write out its incorrect spellings, just to confirm the correct one?)

2. We make surprising discoveries by using surprising methods. (As William Blake said, "If the fool would persist in his folly, he would become wise" and "The road of excess leads to the palace of wisdom.")

3. All words have magical properties that we should experience and explore.

4. Play is healthy.

The first nine exercises below are what might be called the positive side of the nine reading mistakes discussed in Chapter 5. The other exercises are corollaries or extensions of the first nine, or, in some cases, are just bolts from the blue.

1. *Changing single words.* This involves changing one word in a sentence in such a way as to keep the grammar intact but to give the sentence a whole new meaning. The change will sometimes give the old sentence a new sparkle. As Aristotle said, "Aeschuylus and Euripides wrote the same line. . . with the change only of a single word; an unfamiliar word was substituted for an ordinary one, and the new line is beautiful where the old was commonplace" (Dorsch 64).

Take, for example, the way I revised *The Motor Maids across the Continent*, one book in a series of inane novels for adolescent girls. It was written by Katherine Stokes and published in 1911. I found it in a used book shop in 1964. At that time, I was in the habit of making myself read certain books solely because they were the type I would *never* read. It turned out that I wouldn't exactly read *Motor Maids* either, not the way the author had intended, anyway.

The book opens with the preparations for a trip some young girls and their sententious chaperone, Mrs. Wilhelmina Campbell, are to take across the United States by car. Early in their trip, they see a small airplane make a crash landing in a field alongside the highway, and they rush to the aid of the aeroplanist. When he regains consciousness, he finds himself surrounded by the Motor Maids and the redoubtable Mrs. Campbell.

> "Are you better now?" asked Mrs. Campbell, applying her smelling salts to his nose.

With a pencil I marked out *ing salts*, so that the sentence reads,

> "Are you better now?" asked Mrs. Campbell, applying her smell to his nose.

Later the girls load their car with a heavy box of provisions. Something in me clicked, and I changed *provisions* to *visions*. Immediately the book took on a different caste. These young girls were visionaries! And visionaries who kept their visions in a box! The story became immeasurably more interesting. Anytime it lagged a bit, I searched around for another key word and changed it, too. The more I read, the more changes I made, until the Motor Maids found themselves going through a series of mysterious and often humorous adventures.

I went through the entire book this way, and then I typed up my version of *Motor Maids*, which in effect had become a posthumous collaboration with the original author. Later, I revised this new version, following traditional methods and, again, the new method. My friend Ted Berrigan used the same method in creating his novel *Clear the Range*, a metaphysical western.

Of course you don't have to rewrite an entire book. You can just hit here and there. Many authors have pet words they use over and over; it's fun to detect them and substitute another word. Or, if you don't want to be so methodical, simply change a word every once in a while, when the text becomes dull.

Some people will find this procedure jejune or delinquent. They will liken it to drawing a moustache on every face that appears in a magazine or on a billboard. The difference between transforming words and drawing moustaches is that the latter soon loses its appeal and is seen as the visual cliché that it is, whereas the former is infinitely various, because it can be based on widely different texts and it challenges the reader's ingenuity.

A corollary procedure involves a more extensive transformation. Take a brief text (a lyric poem will do nicely) and remove, say, all its nouns. Using any method you want, compile a list of other nouns. From this list, select nouns at random, and, in the order of selection, put them in the vacated noun-slots in the poem. (The Oulipo group in France has long used a similar method, which they call S + 7. The S is an abbreviation for the French word for "noun," and the seven indicates how many nouns down in the dictionary one goes to find a replacement noun.) Read the poem in its new form and see what new sense it makes, if any. You might want to move some of the new nouns around, or even cheat and replace some with others from your noun-horde. When the new version seems to cohere, consider it finished. Then go back and read the original poem again. You will now have a far better sense of it.

The sudden clarity with which we see the original text is similar to what Wolfgang Iser calls "a kind of 'awakening'" when we put down an engrossing book (*The Act of Reading* 104). Engaged reading involves an "image-building process . . . whose significance lies in the fact that image-building eliminates the subject–object division essential for all perception, so that when we 'awaken' to the real world, this division seems all the more accentuated . . . so that we can view our own world as a thing 'freshly understood'" (140). (I remember, as a child, having the raw realness of the world laid bare every time I walked out of a movie theater into the shockingly bright afternoon.) The image-building that is required by the noun substitution process takes us one step away from the "reality" of the original text, to which our return is a kind of awakening.

The substitution procedure can be done with the verbs, adjectives, adverbs, conjunctions, and prepositions. If you try substituting for each of these parts of speech, you will notice that each part-of-speech category changes the poem in a different way. The nouns and verbs alter the original poem far more than the others. If you change only the conjunctions or the prepositions, you might find that the poem could still pass as being by the original author, whereas radical changes in the verbs and nouns immediately "show," provided the original text is well known. "Lord, Lord, why hast thou disconnected me?" (The Bible) exhibits obvious tampering, whereas the alteration in "Rage, rage behind the dying in the light" (Dylan Thomas) isn't so obvious. As you can see, the procedure is wide open, to be taken as far as you want. And often, the farther you go, the clearer the original text is when you come back to it.

2. *Alternate lines.* Read every other line of any text. To help the mind not succumb to the temptation of "normal" reading, and to help the eyes find every other line easily, pull a ruler or piece of paper down as you read. Some texts are just as dull read this way as when read in the usual manner, but others lend themselves marvelously to fresh combinations of ideas and images, many of them comical. If this approach doesn't seem to "work" at first, be patient. One's mind can be deeply grooved in the usual reading pattern, so that initially any other pattern will seem tiring and pointless. If you keep reading alternate lines with no interesting moments or satisfaction at all, try another text, perhaps something lighter, such as magazine prose. How-to articles often become very funny when read this way.

3. *Line looping.* Read every line at least twice. If it's too hard to do silently, do it aloud, which will bring out the rhythm and euphony of the words. In fact, with some texts this can raise the material almost to the level of song. I'm thinking particularly of the blues, in which the first line of each verse is always repeated, then followed by a different line:

> In the evenin', in the evenin', momma, when the sun go down,
> In the evenin', in the evenin', Lord, when the sun go down,
> Yes it's lonesome, so lonesome, when the one you love is not
> around.

You might want to try writing a song in blues form by combining methods 1 (changing single words) and 3 (line looping). Select a text with lines that, when repeated, sound good to you. It's more interesting to work with unlikely material, such as sports writing or a society column, than with, say, greeting cards. (The lines in newspaper columns may prove to be too short for this. If so, cheat and use a few words from the next line.) Pick out the repeated lines, then add the final line, in which you change the last word so that it rhymes with the repeated lines. Or change the final word of the repeated lines so that it rhymes with the last line of each verse. Here are two examples, developed from the *New York Times*:

An ancient white magic has proved itself once again
An ancient white magic has proved itself once again
And water has made us very thin

Tastes in dance were equally specific
Tastes in dance were equally specific
In 1948, the vogue was for the psychologically terrific

Whether or not you want to go to such lengths—in effect switching the act of reading into the act of writing—you'll find that by looping lines you'll begin to get a better feel for the material's rhythm. All strings of words have rhythm. They may not have a regular thump-de-thump kind of rhythm—meter—but they will have a rhythmical contour, with pauses, staccato skips, or longer, more limber phrases. Some lines will be quick; others, cumbersome, clompy, or lurching. All these characteristics, good and bad, tend to go unnoticed when we read for content, whether in fiction or nonfiction, and yet they form the underpinnings of how we feel about what we read. By isolating a group of words, line looping provides a simple way to perceive those underpinnings.

After trying line looping for a while, read a work by Gertrude Stein, particularly one that is based on the rhythms of repetition, such as "As a Wife Has a Cow: A Love Story" (543-45). You'll begin to find that difficult works of literature, such as Stein's, aren't so difficult after all, because once you feel comfortable with an author's cadences, the work tends to reveal itself.

4. *Transposing (up or down).* The most basic form of this procedure is to bring a word from the previous line down into the one you're reading, or to bring one up from the next line. As discussed in Chapter 5, this can happen spontaneously when two similar words appear one above the other. It can also happen spontaneously when a word catches the eye, particularly a charged word, such as sex. Just a moment ago, did you see the word sex when you were still reading a line above the line it's in? (I intentionally didn't italicize it.) If sex doesn't get your attention, your own name is almost certain to. On the other hand, we almost never transpose the so-called service words (*the*, *a*, *an*, *of*, *in*, *etc.*), which are practically inert.

Transposing words up and down *at will*, however, is rather more difficult, because doing so is contrary to old visual habits. Even if you can transpose at will, it's probably easier for you to go down and get a word than to go up and get one: or, having gone down to the next line, the temptation is simply to go on from there. If transposing up and down proves too hard at first, let your eyes drop from line to line, like a series of little waterfalls in a mountain stream, as in Figures 9 and 10, both of

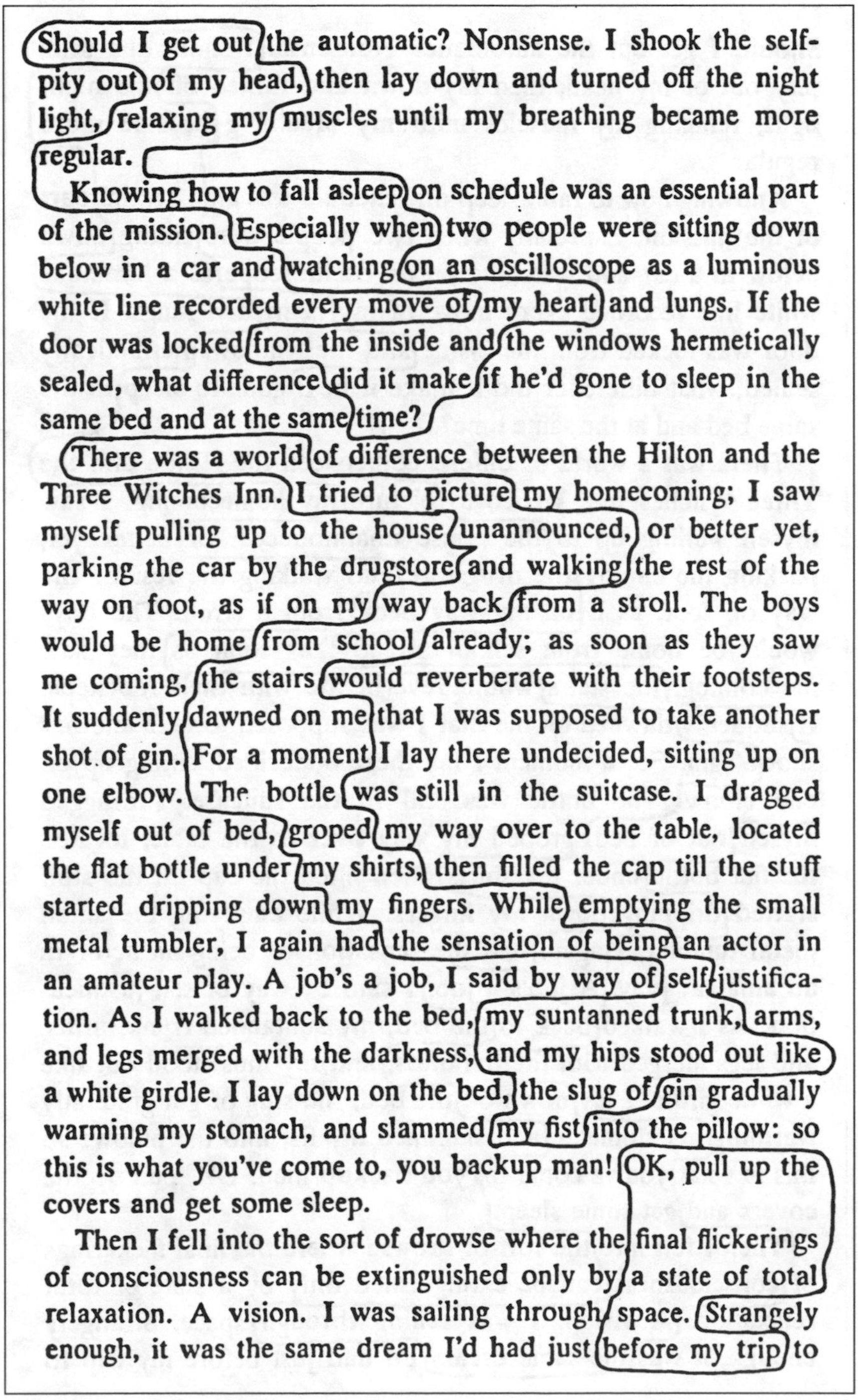

Should I get out the automatic? Nonsense. I shook the self-pity out of my head, then lay down and turned off the night light, relaxing my muscles until my breathing became more regular.

Knowing how to fall asleep on schedule was an essential part of the mission. Especially when two people were sitting down below in a car and watching on an oscilloscope as a luminous white line recorded every move of my heart and lungs. If the door was locked from the inside and the windows hermetically sealed, what difference did it make if he'd gone to sleep in the same bed and at the same time?

There was a world of difference between the Hilton and the Three Witches Inn. I tried to picture my homecoming; I saw myself pulling up to the house unannounced, or better yet, parking the car by the drugstore and walking the rest of the way on foot, as if on my way back from a stroll. The boys would be home from school already; as soon as they saw me coming, the stairs would reverberate with their footsteps. It suddenly dawned on me that I was supposed to take another shot of gin. For a moment I lay there undecided, sitting up on one elbow. The bottle was still in the suitcase. I dragged myself out of bed, groped my way over to the table, located the flat bottle under my shirts, then filled the cap till the stuff started dripping down my fingers. While emptying the small metal tumbler, I again had the sensation of being an actor in an amateur play. A job's a job, I said by way of self-justification. As I walked back to the bed, my suntanned trunk, arms, and legs merged with the darkness, and my hips stood out like a white girdle. I lay down on the bed, the slug of gin gradually warming my stomach, and slammed my fist into the pillow: so this is what you've come to, you backup man! OK, pull up the covers and get some sleep.

Then I fell into the sort of drowse where the final flickerings of consciousness can be extinguished only by a state of total relaxation. A vision. I was sailing through space. Strangely enough, it was the same dream I'd had just before my trip to

Figure 9. Trickle down example 1.

Should I get out the automatic? Nonsense. I shook the self-pity out of my head, then lay down and turned off the night light, relaxing my muscles until my breathing became more regular.

Knowing how to fall asleep on schedule was an essential part of the mission. Especially when two people were sitting down below in a car and watching on an oscilloscope as a luminous white line recorded every move of my heart and lungs. If the door was locked from the inside and the windows hermetically sealed, what difference did it make if he'd gone to sleep in the same bed and at the same time?

There was a world of difference between the Hilton and the Three Witches Inn. I tried to picture my homecoming; I saw myself pulling up to the house unannounced, or better yet, parking the car by the drugstore and walking the rest of the way on foot, as if on my way back from a stroll. The boys would be home from school already; as soon as they saw me coming, the stairs would reverberate with their footsteps. It suddenly dawned on me that I was supposed to take another shot of gin. For a moment I lay there undecided, sitting up on one elbow. The bottle was still in the suitcase. I dragged myself out of bed, groped my way over to the table, located the flat bottle under my shirts, then filled the cap till the stuff started dripping down my fingers. While emptying the small metal tumbler, I again had the sensation of being an actor in an amateur play. A job's a job, I said by way of self-justification. As I walked back to the bed, my suntanned trunk, arms, and legs merged with the darkness, and my hips stood out like a white girdle. I lay down on the bed, the slug of gin gradually warming my stomach, and slammed my fist into the pillow: so this is what you've come to, you backup man! OK, pull up the covers and get some sleep.

Then I fell into the sort of drowse where the final flickerings of consciousness can be extinguished only by a state of total relaxation. A vision. I was sailing through space. Strangely enough, it was the same dream I'd had just before my trip to

Figure 10. Trickle down example 2.

which are based on Stanislaw Lem's novel, *Chain of Chance* "Trickle down" reading is harder than it looks here. I had to search a bit to find a plausible example, and I've made it easier by marking a pattern for you.

This pattern is similar to what typesetters and proofreaders call "rivers," those runs of white space between words that sometimes are so aligned atop each other that a "river" of white seems to run down the page. At some point in your reading, you've probably noticed such rivers; they tend to jump out suddenly, the way a knot in a board suddenly resembles the profile of, say, Abraham Lincoln, or the way a cloud abruptly becomes a dog. Look at Figure 11 for an example of a river. Notice that if you tilt the top of the page down toward the floor a bit and sight along it from bottom to top, the vertical river along the left-hand side of the example becomes even more obvious. Of course, this example is contrived for effect: natural typographic rivers, like aquatic ones, meander here and there.

> the best way to see the world is on foot, whereby
> the pace of the traveler is slowed so that the
> eye is able to take in every little detail, all
> the tiny, wonderful moments otherwise lost. This is
> but one reason for slowing one's pace, for there
> are many others, not the least of which is that
> pot of gold that glimmers brightly and powerfully at
> the end of the rainbow of the emotions, the great
> pot known as inner peace. In order to reach it,
> one must do more than walk very slowly, of course,
> and walking slowly does not guarantee that even
> the most well-intentioned seeker will be able to find
> out what so many have sought to learn: whether or
> not heaven or nirvana can be equated with inner
> pax and whether or not the external, spiritual one, in
> any sense other than strictly metaphoric.

Figure 11. A "river."

5. *Edge blur.* In edge blur, the edges of a page of type are blurred, but the center portion of each line is kept in focus. Figure 12 gives an idea of the areas involved.

The corollary method is center blur, in which only the left- and right-hand parts of each line are read. This corollary method is a good corrective for people whose fixations at the beginnings and ends of lines are

Teachers & Writers Collaborative (T&W) announces an **Outreach Program** to build connections to and a forum for writers, educators, students, parents, and others concerned with the art of writing.

T&W is a nonprofit organization formed in 1967 in New York City. Our program has three components: 1) sending writers into schools and community settings to teach writing and work with teachers; 2) publishing a magazine, books, and other materials about teaching imaginative writing, which we distribute to a national audience; and 3) hosting seminars, lectures, workshops, readings, and other events in our Center for Imaginative Writing.

Our goals for the **Outreach Program** are broad. On the one hand, we are trying to link up with groups and people who already share our ideas about teaching writing. On the other hand, we are seeking opportunities to influence and learn from those with different approaches. We seek new contributors to our publications and a new audience for our materials.

T&W will work with educators or others to design a program that meets their needs. Depending on available resources, T&W can provide the following services and materials:

• T&W has a cadre of professional writers who have taught writing to students of all ages. These writers are available to give presentations, to teach demonstration classes, and to work individually or in groups with teachers, students, or others interested in the problems of teaching writing. Our writers are primarily poets and fiction writers—though most have also written essays and articles—who represent diverse styles and approaches to writing and teaching.

• T&W issues a publications catalogue that lists all the materials we publish and the related books we distribute. We can provide catalogues to groups and individuals interested in this selective collection of materials for teaching writing.

• T&W publishes *Teachers & Writers* magazine five time a year, in addition to our more than 60 professional books for teachers of writing. We also distribute other materials, such as creative books for kids and audio-visual tapes. T&W can set up displays of these materials and, as part of certain Outreach Programs, provide participants with T&W publications.

• T&W's administrative staff includes people with many years of experience setting up writing programs, negotiating contracts with the public schools, and editing and publishing children's writing and professional books for educators. T&W administrators are available to work with people interested in developing programs and publications.

• T&W is also open to inventive collaborations other than those outlined above. If you have ideas or questions, please call T&W at (212) 691-6590.

Figure 12. Edge blur.

hasty. Edge and center blur are related to the stencil method (see #14 below).

6. *Page skips.* This is one of the easier creative reading methods. All you have to do is read a page, flip at random to another page, read it, flip to another, and so on. It's easier than some of the other methods because it leaves large chunks (whole pages) of syntax intact. In any kind of reading, the mind *craves* meaning; meaning is systematically subverted when you read using any of methods 1–5. The mind tends to try to repair the shattered meaning by guessing at its original form or inventing a new context in which the syntactical fragments make at least some sense. Page skipping doesn't require these frequent mental efforts, because the textual breaks come after longer intervals.

Fiction lends itself particularly well to page skipping. You can turn just about any novel into what might be loosely called a Cubist version of itself. By page skipping back and forth at random, you abolish the novel's time line: its events no longer go from point A forward to point Z. Flashbacks and flashforwards take on the same weight as the present, because past, present, and future are abolished, and then united in a sort of eternal present. Likewise, the novel's characters are glimpsed in fragments, then combined by the memory to form mental sketches or portraits.

You can buy such novels ready-made. Unwittingly, the authors of the Hardy Boys and Nancy Drew stories have created cubistic narratives in their series of "branching" novels. A branching novel is one in which the story starts normally, then comes to a point at which the reader has the option of several lines of narrative development. For example, in *The Secret of the Knight's Sword* by Carolyn Keene and Franklin W. Dixon (the first of their "Be a Detective" Mystery Stories), a legend has it that if anything happens to the "Silver Knight," a suit of armor that stands in the Bromley Hall mansion, the family will be cursed. The Hardy Boys and Nancy Drew accompany Nancy's father, Carson Drew, to Bromley Hall, where he has been summoned.

In Chapter 1, the characters are on their way to Bromley Hall when they notice a mysterious green car speeding past them, and as they enter the Bromley Hall driveway, they pass a Rolls-Royce whose driver looks nervous. Once inside the mansion, they learn that the Silver Knight's sword has been stolen! At the bottom of page 5, the reader is given three options:

1. To have Nancy Drew and the Hardy Boys stay at Bromley Hall and investigate. If so, turn to page 6 and continue.

2. Have them follow the trail of the green car. If so, turn to page 10 and continue.

3. Have them investigate the driver of the Rolls-Royce. If so, turn to page 12 and continue.

The entire book has 18 of these branching points and 17 different endings (the first on page 42 and the last on page 122, the book's final page). So if you follow instructions, you can get 17 different narratives from this one book.

But if you read the book straight through, you'll find even more interesting things happening. Early on, young Elizabeth Bromley walks in and asks what's going on. A statue falls from the top of the stairway and narrowly misses her. She is so shaken that she's taken off to her room. Immediately she walks in the door again and asks what's going on. The Hardy Boys and Nancy tell her the sword's been stolen, they discuss the green car, investigate, and head toward London. Elizabeth Bromley walks in the door and asks what's going on. The Hardy Boys and Nancy explain that the sword's been stolen and tell her about the driver of the Rolls-Royce. The three young detectives follow the car's trail to Kent. But on the next page they are still at Bromley Hall, investigating the garden. And so on.

Branching novels might be seen as a twentieth-century descendent of serial novels. Wolfgang Iser says that "readers in the nineteenth century. . . often found a novel read in installments to be better than the very same novel in book form." He explains that

> the difference arises out of the cutting technique used in the serial story. It generally breaks off just at a point of suspense where one would like to know the outcome of a meeting, a situation, etc. The interruption and consequent prolongation of tension is the basic function of the cut. The result is that we try to imagine how the story will unfold, and in this way we heighten our own participation in the course of events. Dickens was a master of the technique; his readers became his "co-authors." (1978, 191)

Branching novels were more directly inspired, I suspect, by the narrative options in board games such as Dungeons and Dragons and the flow charts of computer programming. The process came full circle when novelist Thomas M. Disch wrote *Amnesia*, a branching novel for computer; it comes on diskette and is highly reader-interactive. Whatever their origin, branching novels have proved to be surprisingly popular. Bantam claims that its "Choose Your Own Adventure" series alone has sold more than 32,000,000 copies since its inception in 1979.

People with intellectual curiosity naturally "branch-read" the dictionary. We read the definition of one word, and something in the definition suggests another word, so we look it up, and so on. Or, in looking up one word, we happen to notice another, which may lead to the one next to it, and so on. This leisurely, pleasant, seemingly haphazard careening around in the dictionary has two "engines" that keep it going: meaning and contiguity.

The skipping method can be used with larger chunks, such as episodes or chapters. It can also be made to follow a pattern of first, last, second, next-to-last, third, third-to-last, and so on, whether applied to whole pages, episodes, or chapters. For instance, you could read a novel's first chapter, its last, its second, its next-to-last, and so on, until you end—in the middle of the book.

When I was a young boy, my family and I would go to the movies without knowing the show times. We'd arrive in the middle of a movie, see it to the end, stay for the intermission, then watch the movie from the beginning, until that magic moment of recognition when one of us would say, "This is where we came in." It seems odd that we did this with such impunity, but at the time it seemed perfectly normal, even when the two parts of the movie were separated by another entire movie—the other half of a double feature. We were still able to reassemble the two halves of the first film. It was only when I got older and became interested in movies as "art" that I insisted on seeing movies from opening credits to The End, and although at this point I was bringing a lot more conscious attention to my movie viewing, I don't think I was enjoying the movies any more than before,

In 1962, *Editions du Seuil* published an unusual French novel, *Composition #1* by Marc Sappora. The novel came in a book-sized box, with the pages inside unbound and unnumbered. The reader was instructed to shuffle the pages and read them in random order. Then, of course, shuffle them again.

Composition #1 might have been inspired by Raymond Queneau's *Cent mille milliards de poèmes (One Hundred Trillion Poems)*. Queneau's collection consists of 10 sonnets, which he calls "generator sonnets." The book is designed so that the reader can turn not a page at a time, but a line at a time. To get an idea of what it looks like, imagine a book of matches opened and turned on its side, with the match heads on the right-hand side. If you want to see a match below, you simply bend back the one above it. The same for the lines in Queneau's poems. So, if you wish to replace the first line of the first poem, simply turn it, the way you would a page (or match), and expose the first line of the second sonnet. The possible permutations of the 140 lines of the generator sonnets allow for the creation of 1,000,000,000,000 poems, in only 10 pages! Queneau estimates that it would take approximately 200,000,000 years to read all those poems, assuming, of course, you read 24 hours a day. Incidentally, he says his collection was inspired by a children's book called *Têtes de rechange*, in which various heads could be put on various bodies. Such books are still available in the U.S.

Queneau and Sappora's shuffling of lines and pages recalls the exaggerated use of multiple parentheses by Raymond Roussel in his narrative poem, "New Impressions of Africa."[1] Here I'll give (though less through the generosity of my heart ((which has been beating normally lately (((although I have no idea of what "normally" is ;((((well, maybe I do)))) in a case like mine))) and much to my relief)) than through sheer perversity) an example of how difficult, if not impossible, it is to read multiply parenthetical sentences without skipping back and forth.[2]

But let's skip back to page skipping. The most natural form of page skipping is in collections of poetry. In fact, one of the reasons I like reading books of poetry is that they allow you to skip around in them. You can read the poems in any order you want. I often read the first poem, then the last, then the shorter ones, then the rest. Only after I've bounced around this way do I go back and read the entire book from start to finish, and then only if the book is worth reading again.

Reading poetry collections from start to finish assumes that someone—the author, perhaps—arranged the poems in a particular sequence for specific reasons, an assumption that is not always true. Often the poems were written at different times, in different moods, and on different subjects, and are meant to be discrete units. Their proximity between the covers of a book is simply a bow to the convention of traditional book binding. I remember having long, detailed discussions with poet Ted Berrigan in the early 1960s about John Ashbery's book of poems, *The Tennis Court Oath*. Ted and I saw the same rich and complex mind at work in establishing the sequence of the poems as the one involved in writing them in the first place. When we met Ashbery and commented on his careful arrangement, he replied, "Oh, I just sent a bunch of poems to the editor and he did the rest." Ted and I, who took great and sometimes ludicrous pains in arranging our own poems in structured sequences, were surprised by Ashbery's willingness to see his poems arranged in any order, though that in fact is how we ourselves read most poetry books—in effect creating our own notion of the architecture of each book.

Ted and I also used another method to rearrange a text: reading it backwards one word at a time. Just as running backwards improves one's physical agility, reading backwards improves one's mental agility. Ted and I used the backwards method for both reading and writing. For writing purposes, one of us would read any text aloud backward to the other, who was poised at the typewriter, mixing the unusual flow of words with our own inner flow.

Reading specialist Jeanne Chall used a similar method when she took a page from an ordinary reading primer and read it from bottom to top (one sentence at a time). Not surprisingly, she found that the text had "more punch" read backwards than when read forward (*Learning to Read*, 96). Another language authority, Ann E. Berthoff, says that we can focus more intently on particular sentences if we read backwards (also one sentence at a time). Her remarks deal with correcting one's own prose writing, but the effect is the same: the "sentences sound alien, like those in a workbook, and for the purposes of correction, that is all to the good" (191). In reading backwards, that alien sound is exactly what I'm looking for, because it's this feeling of differentness that activates one's feeling for the magical nature of words.

   7. *Page repeats.* Repeats are akin both to line loops and page skips—line loops because page repeats are simply larger units than line repeats, and page skipping because it's always possible (and even likely, considering how a book's binding will often cause a book to fall open to the same pages) you'll happen to turn to the same page again.

   To read each page of a book twice before going on to the next page is a massive form of eye regression (discussed in Chapter 5). I've never read an entire book this way, although I frequently go back and read large chunks of material that is intellectually demanding. I think I would have a hard time reading each page twice in a book I didn't particularly like, and in one I did particularly like I'd just want to forge ahead.

   It's rather pleasant, though, to skip around in a novel and happen upon a page you've already read. If you're skipping at random to create your own Cubist version of the novel, these repeats take on a lyrical quality, something like that of the pantoum form in poetry, wherein the lines come back, as in:

> Because birds are gliding across your brain,
> I rise into the shadows
> And the mist is rolling in
> Because my breath is rolling out.
>
> I rise into the shadows
> Like a pond that went to sleep:
> Because my breath is rolling out
> You hear doorbells in the woods.
>
> Like a pond that went to sleep
> And woke up inside a dream,
> You hear doorbells in the woods
> Though the woods are in the dream
>
> And woke up inside a dream!
> Although the air is filled with blue and white clouds,

Though the woods are in the dream,
A good idea can smell like pine trees.

Although the air is filled with blue and white clouds,
I am filled with ideas about dreams
A good idea can smell like pine trees
And a dream can grow like a cloud.

I am filled with ideas about dreams,
The stars don't know what they mean
And a dream can grow like a cloud:
You can't explain this bigness.

The stars don't know what they mean
And the mist is rolling in.
You can't explain this bigness
Because birds are gliding across your brain.

A similar thing happens in the novels of Alain Robbe-Grillet (such as *The Voyeur* and *Jealousy*) and in his screenplays (such as *Last Year at Marienbad*), in which certain images and phrases are repeated at various points in the story, like a refrain. Here's a nutshell example from *The Voyeur:*

It was the last house as he left town. Madame Leduc had opened the door almost at once. The preliminaries had gone very fast: the brother working for the steamship line, the wrist watches at prices defying all competition, the hallway splitting the house down the middle, the door to the right, the big kitchen, the oval table in the middle of the room, the oilcloth with the many-colored little flowers, the pressure of his fingers on the suitcase clasp, the cover opening back, the black memorandum book, the prospectuses, the rectangular frame on top of the sideboard, the shiny metal support, the photograph, the sloping path, the hollow on the cliff sheltered from the wind, secret, calm, isolated as if by thick walls . . . as if by thick walls . . . the oval table in the middle of the room, the oilcloth with the many-colored little flowers, the pressure of his fingers on the suitcase clasp, the cover opening back as if on a spring, the black memorandum book, the prospectuses, the shiny metal frame, the photograph showing . . . the photograph showing the photograph, the photograph, the photograph, the photograph. . . . (98)

8. *Eye–Mind Split.* One of the least productive things you can do—in terms of traditional reading—is to let your mind wander. Your eyes keep moving along the words while your mind moves elsewhere. How many times were you exhorted as a child, "Pay attention!"? But pay attention to what? When *my* mind wanders, it's usually paying attention, but to something else. In creative reading, wandering is used as a positive technique that puts the reader in closer touch with where the mind is when it wanders and what it does there.

In eye–mind split reading, the mind may be likened to a water-skier, the words to water. The mind flies along the surface, bouncing a bit in the rough going. But what's that up ahead? It's a ramp. The skier heads straight for it, glides up the inclined plane, and shoots out into the air in a smooth arc that rises and then falls to the point of reestablishing contact with the water. In reading, be alert for these ramps in the text. They might be individual words, particular turns of phrase, names of places or people, dates, descriptions, or scenes—anything that can send you off into a memory or fantasy.

Such ramps transport me when, for example, a cashier announces that the sum total of my purchases is seventeen seventy-six, nineteen twenty-nine, or nineteen forty-two (the year I was born). Sometimes I respond with a remark based on what I have intentionally misunderstood to be such a date in history. For 1929, I might say something like "Gee, that was a bad year. I lost all my money and can't pay." These utterances usually provoke blank looks from the sales personnel, who are not accustomed, as Walter Pater put it, to having "the ornamental word, the figure, the accessory form or color or reference . . . stirring a long 'brainwave' behind it of perhaps quite alien association" (Iser 1978, 126). In the privacy of your own home, however, and with book in hand, you can take these associative leaps without disconcerting a hapless interlocutor.

The trick is to keep your eyes moving along the book's words at the same time as your mind has gone off on its "trip," and then to return from the trip and make a fairly smooth landing on the words again. This is a bit harder than simply going off on a fantasy, because it involves your creating a segue (or "bridge") between your fantasy and the words as you reenter the text.

Sometimes English teachers assign corollary methods. For instance, they have their students read a descriptive passage, and close their eyes to try to "see" what they've just read, to create a vivid and detailed mental picture of the description. Afterward, when students compare their mental pictures, they're surprised by both the similarities and the differences. The creation of static mental pictures is something the students have done naturally from an early age but rarely if ever acknowledged publicly, sometimes not even privately.

Some teachers also have their students read the beginning of a story, then stop and invent the rest. To do this well, the students have to project themselves *into* the story—in order to move it forward in a plausible line of development—the way they have to project themselves into a static mental picture.

Such exercises in imagination are fine; I've done them many times myself. I've read the first chapter of a novel, stopped, and projected ahead; read the second chapter, stopped, and revised my projection; read the third chapter, stopped, and revised my projection again; and so on. Sometimes I make a final projection after the last chapter; in other words, I keep the story going beyond the end of the book.

Eye-mind split is a bit different. It involves drifting off on a tangent, with no pretense of honoring the story's logic. Also, eye-mind split often happens when the reader's eyes are still open and moving along the words on the page. Finally, it requires that at some point the reader realize that he or she is off on a tangent and must now bend that tangent back so that it segues nicely into the material being read at that moment. As you might suspect, it's easier to go off on a tangent than to come back on one. It's perfectly all right to go off, then snap back and abruptly start reading the "real" words again. It just isn't as elegant as reentering the text smoothly. In either case, becoming mindful of eye-mind split helps us to control it—either to let ourselves go or to hew close to the printed text—and thus become better and more creative readers.

9. *Column confusion.* Column confusion, you may recall from Chapter 5, consists of errors in reading a column of type in a newspaper or magazine.

Column confusion happens sometimes when we get to the end of one column of a magazine or newspaper article and go on to what we think is the next column, but which actually belongs to a different article. Sometimes this mistake is induced by material that is poorly designed and laid out.

We can capitalize on this type of column confusion by simply doing it on purpose. Take, for example, the front page of your daily newspaper. Read it, column by column, beginning in the upper left-hand corner, continuing straight down to the bottom of the page, even (and especially) if it means breaking into other articles. Then go up to the top of the second column and read it all the way down to the bottom of the page. Then up to the third, and so on, until you end up at the bottom right-hand corner of the page.

A less usual form of column confusion is one used for literary purposes by novelist William S. Burroughs. He calls it "reading cross-column." To read cross-column, all you do is read from left to right, pretending

One of the things	Of great beauty
that makes Paris a	joy, and certainly a
traveler's nightmare	bonus to life, he
is the intolerance	and perhaps you,
Parisians show to	considering how the
foreigners trying to	narrow and really
speak French. All too	human quality of
often the tourist	will that he
goes away swearing	and I share
never to return	just a little bit

Figure 13. Two columns example.

there's no dividing line between the columns. For example, try reading the two columns in Figure 13 this way (so that the first line reads "One of the things of great beauty").

Of course this is an example whose grammar permits relatively smooth sailing across the columns.[3] The syntactical waters are somewhat choppier in columns that are pasted up wherever they happen to fit, with little or no regard to adjacent columns—the message being, of course, that you aren't *supposed* to read cross-column. Sometimes I've wondered, though, if there might not be a devilish paste-up artist who, every once in a while, secretly matches up two disparate columns so that they yield a shocking or unusual image, an image no one ever notices.

Reading cross-column works particularly well between two or three columns, producing what are called "cut-ups" (but because the cutting is done with the eye, there's no muss, no fuss, you don't need scissors or paste). Reading all the way across six or eight columns usually produces such a syntactical mess among so many different subjects that we soon tire of it. It's chaotic. Best to start with cutting across just two columns.

Take the fragment in Figure 14, clipped from the front page of the *New York Times* (Sunday, July 6, 1986). The first column contains an article about airport security measures designed to thwart terrorism; the second column is about the reopening of the refurbished Statue of Liberty; the third, fourth, and fifth columns tell about visitors to the newly opened

"All the News That's Fit to Print"

The New York Times

VOL.CXXXV .... No. 46,827

NEW YORK, SUNDAY, JULY 6, 1986

$1.25

Weather: Hazy sunshine, hot and humid today; hazy and warm tonight. Continued hazy and humid tomorrow. Temperatures today 90-95, tonight 73; 77; yesterday 68-90. Details, page 23.

Miss Liberty Reopens Amid Gaiety in the Harbor

Contests, Concerts and Street Festival Entertain Crowds

By ROBERT D. McFADDEN

A refurbished Statue of Liberty was reopened to the public yesterday as the Liberty Weekend party, hardly pausing on the morning after, rolled ahead with boat and air races, open houses aboard berthed ships and a huge festival in lower Manhattan.

It was a patchwork quilt day: banjos and fiddles reverberated on Wall Street, experts conferred on liberty's meaning, families explored the mysteries of binnacles and topgallants, classical music drifted in the parks and sailors in dress-whites were on the town.

But it was again the Statue of Liberty, symbol of a nation and the centerpiece of a harbor teeming with ships and sails, that captured the day, ending a two-year centennial restoration to its 19th century grandeur and reopening to visitors for the first time in a year.

Mrs. Reagan Cuts Ribbon

Associated Press

FOES OF APARTHEID SEEK OUT AND KILL 5 BLACK OFFICIALS

SHOOTINGS IN TOWNSHIPS

South Africa Says 2 Gunmen, Seeking Targets From Car, Die in Fight With Police

Special to The New York Times

JOHANNESBURG, July 5 — Anti-Government gunmen armed with Soviet designed AK-47 assault rifles shot and killed five black municipal officials early today, the authorities said.

Two of the assailants, reportedly driving through segregated black townships in search of targets, were said to have been killed by the police after a high-speed car chase.

The attacks seemed to be among the most audacious guerrilla assaults on black supporters of Government authority since the current unrest began

Figure 14. Front page of the *New York Times*.

statue; and the sixth column is about the anti-apartheid struggle in South Africa. Pick any two columns and read them from left to right, ignoring their dividing line. Don't worry if the syntactical jumps between them aren't smooth, or if the lines do not line up perfectly.

Any surprises? Giving it a quick scan, I found several. Right away I got "The nation's major airports are a bouquet of white roses" (columns 1 and 2). This sentence is delightful for its fresh mixture of two types of diction—the dry, official "nation's major airports" joined with the more lyrical "bouquet of white roses." It is also delightful and surprisingly apt as an image: airports do have a lot of white in them, and, to extend the metaphor, the planes that buzz and fly around them are like birds or insects. Also in this sentence is the pleasure of imagining these sprawling, massive complexes as something you can hold in one hand, as well as the pleasure of imagining something lifeless and uninteresting (such as concrete) becoming sensuous and beautiful, the way life should be.

I also noticed an inadvertently funny moment in columns 5 and 6, from which I got "As Mr. Weisman and others waited, Mrs. Reagan took an oversized scissors. Meanwhile, Bishop Desmond M. and—with some difficulty because the Tutu, winner of the 1984 Nobel Peace shears, was stiff, cut through a ban and a prominent foe of apartheid." This fragment is syntactically jagged, but consider some of its suggestions. It sounds as though the First Lady, using special scissors that had been awarded the Nobel Peace Prize, is about to cut some material to make a ballet costume (a tutu), but instead she cuts through a ban (such as those imposed on group gatherings) and then keeps snipping away until she accidentally cuts in half "a foe of apartheid"! This mixing of news stories resembles the mixing of people or places in dreams, and, as in dreams, often results in the liberation of feelings and meanings that otherwise remain below the surface, undiscovered and unacknowledged.

Glancing at the paper again, I see some interesting intersections between columns 2 and 3: "It was a steamy, sticky day, with about 4,000 tourists and New Yorkers, temperatures in the low 90s and high in a queue that snaked through thin clouds that sometimes hid a pale Battery Park for the noon ferry to Lib Sun." This sounds like a scene in a science fiction novel, in which a spiral of people goes up into the sky to a spacecraft that will take them to a distant star called Lib Sun.

In these three examples, I've doctored the original source a little by smoothing over the bumpy transitions, leaving out a word or syllable here and there, and avoiding those lines that don't seem to *want* to go together. As Burroughs says, "You learn to leave out words and to make connections," as he does in this demonstration:

> Now, for example, if I wanted to make a cut-up of this (picking up
> a copy of *The Nation*), there are many ways I could do it. I could
> read cross-column; I could say: "Today's men's nerves surround us.
> Each technological extension gone outside is electrical involves an
> act of collective environment. The human nervous environment
> system itself can be reprogrammed with all its private and social
> values because it is content. He programs logically as readily as any
> radio net is swallowed by the new environment. The sensory
> order." You find it often makes quite as much sense as the original.
> (Interview in *Paris Review* 25)

Sometimes a picture for one article can be paired with a different
article. In the upper left-hand corner of the *Times* example, there is a
photograph of tennis player Martina Navratilova celebrating a moment of
victory at Wimbledon. The small caption tells us to read about it in Section 5, which is the sports section. At a distance, though, all I am able to
read under the picture is "Airport Security Slows Travelers." If you've ever
had to wait in long lines at airports, you will have wanted to throw up
your hands and scream, just as Navratilova seems to be doing. She just
couldn't take those long lines at the security check-points.

Coincidentally, another interpretation suggests itself. A few months
before Wimbledon, Navratilova was detained at an airport security check-
point when agents found a loaded revolver in her handbag. The gun,
which she keeps for *her* security, had inadvertently been packed in the
wrong suitcase by a friend. Again, when Navratilova saw the gun removed
from her carry-on luggage, she must had felt like throwing up her hands.

Such juxtapositions are coincidental. Or are they? Isn't it possible
that the paste-up artist recalled, perhaps unconsciously, the airport inci-
dent, and when Navratilova made the news again by winning Wimbledon,
"happened" to put her picture next to an article about airport security?
Burroughs, among others, believes that such juxtapositions (or "intersections") are hardly coincidental, that they have an oracular power, that

> when you make cut-ups you do not simply get random juxtaposi-
> tions of words, that they do mean something, and often these
> meanings refer to some future event. I've made many cut-ups and
> then later recognized that the cut-up referred to something that I
> read later in a newspaper or a book, or something that happened. .
> . . Perhaps events are pre-written and pre-recorded and when you
> cut the word lines the future leaks out. (Odier 12–13)

If these intersections do have a prophetic power, some newspapers keep it in check. In looking through some old newspapers, I had at
first thought I'd find some good examples of intersections in the local
paper, the *Times–Argus* of Barre–Montpelier, Vermont. I was surprised to

see that the *Times–Argus* was virtually cross-column-proof; it is designed so that every article is contained in its own, discrete box, with plenty of empty space between articles, whose columnar lines rarely match up with those of other articles. This portioning out of information reflects the pace of life in small-town and rural Vermont, where people do not rush about trying to do two or more things at the same time, where people are less subject to the constant bombardment of information than are big-city people. You can read every article in the *Times–Argus* in an hour, whereas you would be overloading your brain to read the entire *New York Times*, with its reportage from all over the world, its notices for movies, plays, art exhibitions, dance and musical performances, etc. The point here is not that one newspaper is better than the other; the point is that one newspaper gives you one view of the world, the other gives you another view, not just by their editorial content, but by their sense of what is important to know, and how much of anything is important to know, and how quickly we should know it. And this sense of importance is conveyed as much by layout and design as by content.

You can learn to adjust your reading method accordingly. In most newspapers, the lead article appears in the upper right-hand corner of the front page. In other words, journalists are making the decisions—as someone must on a newspaper—as to what is the single most important story of the day. We grow up reading the newspaper and assuming that "front-page news" is the most significant, but we ought to challenge this ingrained assumption, and teach our children to challenge it, too.

Until a certain age, I was never bothered by the way newspapers ordered their information. After all, it's only reasonable to put all the sports news together, to group the gossip, horoscopes, and advice columns, and so on. When Picasso died, though, I was agitated to find that the *New York Times* lead article of the day was about a squabble between the mayor of New York City and the governor. Picasso got the same amount of space on page 1, but not the lead position. In effect, the *Times* was telling us that a minor moment in local politics was more significant than the death of one of the geniuses of the twentieth century. The values that led to that judgement seemed way off the mark.

The beauty of reading a newspaper is, of course, that we're free to skip around in it, to read it in any order we want, to assign to it our own order of importance. When I was little, I read the comic strips first; now I usually turn directly to the sports page (partly, I think, to reassure myself that the world hasn't altered in some horrible way overnight. Reading the sports page is like participating in a ritual of the Eternal Return.) Poet John Ashbery reads the obituaries first; artist George Schneeman goes straight to the mutual fund quotations, my wife makes a beeline to the crossword puzzle. Do you have such a pattern? What do you read first? What last? And why?

An interesting exercise in this regard is to make your own front page. Read the daily paper just as you normally would, but as you read, cut out the articles and keep them in that sequence. Then glue them back down (on the front page of an old paper, perhaps), forming your own front page, complete with banner and your lead piece at the top right. This exercise provides a graphic model of your newspaper reading pattern, and demonstrates the degree of control we tacitly surrender to—and take back from—the newspaper's staff. It's a particularly good exercise for showing students how to read a newspaper without letting it impose its view of the world on them.

Only a few years ago, scientists at MIT's Media Lab were working on a telecommunications system that would allow us to select stories from the wire services and create our own electronic newspaper on a personal computer. As Walter Bender, one of the MIT computer scientists, put it, "You become one of the authors . . . or editors yourself. . . . It allows you to dictate what you think is newsworthy."[4] In the meantime, the sudden proliferation of the Internet has allowed us to gain access to wire services, electronic editions of newspapers, and other web sites, and to select from them as we wish, in effect becoming editors of the vast amount of information available on any given day. Unfortunately, when it comes to printing out such a selection in an attractive format, the technology is still rather crude, so that whatever "electronic newspaper" we create is still mainly inside our own heads.

Burroughs's application of cross-column or cut-up reading is not only a defiant and subversive gesture toward the "establishment" that helped make a world he does not approve of, it is also a way of making literature. "You get very interesting juxtapositions. Some of them are useful from a literary point of view" (Odier 12). There's nothing complicated or arcane about Burroughs's method:

> It's not unconscious at all, it's a very definite operation. . . .the simplest way is to take a page, cut it down the middle and across the middle, and then rearrange the four sections. Now that's a very simple form of cut-up if you want to get some idea of one rearrangement of the words on that page. It's quite conscious, there's nothing of automatic writing or unconscious procedure involved here. You don't know what you're going to get. (Odier 12)

Burroughs was not the first to use the cut-up technique. He refers to T. S. Eliot's poem "The Waste Land" as "the first great cut-up collage."[5]

Burroughs also refers to Tristan Tzara's cut-ups and John Dos Passos's use of cut-ups in the "Camera Eye" sequences in his novel *USA*. Writing about Burroughs, Gérard-Georges Lemaire also mentions a similar procedure used by artist Marcel Duchamp:

> Duchamp, in his *Rendez-vous du Dimanche 6 février à lh 3/4 après-midi* placed four apparently unrelated texts in four divisions of a square. Such are the ancestors of this [cut-up] technique . . . yet [these ancestors] made no attempt to establish a new form of readability. (Burroughs and Gysin 14)

As far back as 1920, Tristan Tzara, the dadaist poet, gave us a recipe for cut-ups:

To Make a Dadaist Poem

> Take a newspaper.
> Take some scissors.
> From the newspaper pick an article as long as the poem you
> want to make.
> Cut out the article.
> Then carefully cut out each of the words in the article and
> put them in a bag.
> Shake gently.
> Then take out each piece one at a time.
> Copy the words
> in exactly the same order
> as they came out of the bag.
> The poem will resemble you.
> And now you're an infinitely original writer with a charming
> sensibility, if still not understood by the common people.
>   (64, my translation)

Italian writer and educator Gianni Rodari commented on this method:

> It is possible to compose entire poems using a newspaper and a pair of scissors, even though these poems may not make any sense. And yet there will be a fascinating sense.
>   I do not want to maintain that this is the most useful method for reading a newspaper or that newspapers should be used in schools only to be cut into pieces. Paper is something to be taken seriously. Likewise, the freedom of the press. This game is not intended to bring about disrespect for the printed word, although it can serve to temper the worship of the press as a sacred institution. (24)

And again:

> It seems to me that every single mode of exploring coincidence is good. (25)

I wonder if Tzara knew Lewis Carroll's poem "Poeta Fit, non Nasci-tur," one of whose stanzas goes:

> For first you write a sentence,
>   And then you chop it small;
> Then mix the bits, and sort them out
>   Just as they chance to fall:
> The order of the phrases makes
>   No difference at all.
>
> (Grigson 127)

The speaker in Carroll's poem is ironic, but Tzara's irony is so deadpan that we can't be sure it *is* irony. It is possible that Tzara is saying, in effect, that the world has gone mad, that madness has become normal, and therefore we should now embrace nonsense. T. S. Eliot's sober juxtaposi-tions of seemingly unrelated elements suggests that such a procedure could be used meaningfully in "serious" literature. Burroughs takes it a step further in ascribing oracular power to the cut-up. I tend to agree with all four of these viewpoints, any of which I might adopt when I read cross-column. If the procedure seems frivolous, I try to enjoy it, the way I enjoy good nonsense. If the procedure seems to be telling me something impor-tant or unexpected, I listen. Like some of the other creative reading meth-ods in this book, reading cross-column is like taking a Rorschach test: what you see in it depends on who you are. And tells you who you are.

10. *Fold-ins.* The fold-in method, used by experimental novelists such as Burroughs and Tom Veitch and by poets such as Ted Berrigan, is essentially a variant of reading cross-column (number 9, above). To create a simple fold-in, choose a book you don't mind messing up, perhaps a bat-tered paperback. Open it at random. Fold the left-hand page down the middle. (It doesn't matter whether you fold it forward or backward.) If the book was pasted up and printed consistently, the lines of the folded half page should line up with the lines of the page beneath it, half of which is revealed by the folding. (See Figure 15.)

Now read across the two columns of what is in effect a new page. If you don't like the result, flop the folded page and try the new combina-tions thus formed. Or try folding other pages. Some texts make better fold-ins than others; you might have to try several books to find a good one.

The combining of half pages is similar to bringing together two un-known chemicals. Sometimes nothing happens. Sometimes they give off heat and gas and form a compound. I'm not sure why some fold-ins "click" and others don't. It has something to do with the vocabulary, the syntax, and the type of writing (descriptive, narrative, abstract, concrete,

A NIGHT IN "POTATO" VILLAGE   19

With their few primitive farm ɔishly and said, "Well,
grow potatoes, which barely k we did we must not
was why the place was callec? In case war breaks
    Liberation saved Potato Vill drive simply because
5 other crops and began to cut
other sidelines. But traitor Li a laugh. The severity 5
line caused all the people wit
flock to the cities. The villagght. We won't argue
anybody to keep simple accou We'll straighten it out
10   Having vented his grievanc out a pair of padded
his anger gone. "We're muc r his coat and handed
said. "Chairman Mao has sen
sors — a great event for us far. "Me put on . . . ?" 10
tain gullies."
15   "But you must make strict ly. "You had a pair,
said. "They came here to be oung Lin's feet. Don't
  "Of course. When they first
clumsy. They didn't know a t ld do but accept the
They even had to learn how to d around. "Where is
20 a slip in the snow can make
on its back. Chairman Mao e." He pointed to a 15
lower-middle peasants* with th"
youngsters. We must do our appeared, singing and
live up to his confidence in u ds. They were divided
25 hardship. They said one year ling a sled loaded with
done them more good than s peasant and me, they
                                 "Old secretary!" The 20

———————
   * This is a political term denoting es revealed the status
economic status. These were two stra
in the land reform. In class struggle
peasants are the most reliable allies

Figure 15. Fold-in example.

etc.). A various and colorful vocabulary, a syntax filled with discrete segments, and a concrete narrative should fold-in nicely.

   As with reading cross-column, it helps to "cheat" a bit by smoothing out the jumps between columns, to drop word fragments and other bits that don't fit the flow, and to add small helping words. Or, if you prefer your fold-ins undoctored, if you have the mental stamina to absorb the jolts of all those syntactical breaks, do it that way.

A variation on reading fold-ins is what I call *slots*. Fold a page, as in Figure 15. Read the first half line at the top left. If it doesn't lead smoothly into the first right-hand half line, try continuing it with the second right-hand half line, and so on, down the page. When you find one that does fit, go back up and read the second left-hand half line, and try to match it up with a half line in the right side. And so on, with line three.

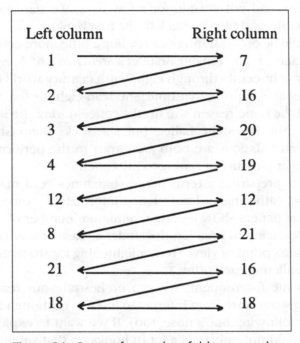

Figure 16. Pattern for reading fold-in example in Figure 15.

Look at Figure 15 again. It shows a page spread from *The Seeds*, a collection of propaganda stories translated from Chinese, with page 17 folded in half, revealing the right half of page 19. I've numbered the lines on each side, left and right. Read the lines in the order indicated in Figure 16. With a minimum of fudging, you might have come up with something like this:

> With their few primitive farms, we'll straighten it out, grow potatoes, which barely appeared, singing, and was why the place was called "Old Secretary"! The Liberation saved the Potato, done them more good than Chairman Mao has said. "They came here to flock to the cities. The village revealed the status on its back." Chairman Mao appeared singing and clumsy. They didn't know a sled loaded with youngsters drives simply because, having vented his grievance, he pointed to a hardship. We won't argue.

That this technique creates great literature, we won't argue. We will argue that it takes a tedious piece of propaganda fiction and sails it off with a little breath of imagination.

11. *Dueling Books.* Dueling books involves reading two books at the same time. Not simultaneously, of course, but alternately. Many of us do this, but rarely with a conscious purpose. We start a book, read a couple of chapters, and put it aside for a few days. We start another book, read it for a while, and then go back to the first book.

We could be orchestrating our reading a little more consciously. My wife, for instance, read Fernand Braudel's *Structures of Everyday Life*, a lengthy study of fifteenth- through eighteenth-century world history, over a period of months. During that time, she read eight or ten mystery novels, for much the same reason she drinks coffee during the intermissions at the ballet. She loves the ballet, but she seeks contrast during the breaks. The intermissions are both a contrast to the performance and a part of the larger pleasure of "going to the ballet."

Students preparing a term paper sometimes read many books at the same time, gathering and correlating information. Some teachers require that term papers show a certain minimum number of sources consulted, the idea being to broaden the students' base of knowledge and to widen the topic's point of view. (It is enlightening for students to find two experts contradicting each other.)

With some forethought, we can orchestrate our reading, rather than just follow our nose from interest to interest (although there is a lot to be said for following one's nose, too). If we want to explore a certain subject, we could not only read a lot of books on that subject, we could also include different genres. It is quite natural to pause in reading a work of nonfiction (such as literary criticism) to read the original material discussed in it, and it is rewarding to read a history of philosophy or religion at the same time as reading the philosophers or theologians themselves. Wide reading gives us a diversity of opinion, but different genres lend a *roundness* to our sense of the subject. For instance, if we're interested in the history of the American Indians, we would do well to add to our reading of history a generous selection of Indian poetry, songs, folk tales, oral histories (such as *Black Elk Speaks*), eyewitness accounts, and diaries. To this we could add recordings of Indian music, pictures of Indian art and craftwork, and documentary photographs—all of which would enrich the orchestration of our reading. It wouldn't hurt to get to know some Indians, and we might even go so far as to camp out in the open for a while.

A more radical and mechanical form of dueling books involves reading them in alternating pages or chapters. It would be interesting to crossbreed, say, Elmore Leonard's novel *Unknown Man No. 89* with Iceberg Slim's *Pimp: The Story of My Life* by reading them alternately page by page. Or Kafka's story "The Hunger Artist" with *The Joy of Cooking*. Or F. Scott Fitzgerald's *Tender Is the Night* and Calvin Tomkins's *Living Well Is the Best Revenge*, a biography of Gerald and Sara Murphy, whom Fitzgerald used as the basis for the main characters of his novel. Or how about crossing Thomas Mann's *Magic Mountain* and a textbook on tuberculosis? The possibilities are unlimited. These crossbreedings produce the sense of a third book, an imaginary hybrid hovering somewhere between the two. This third book is one that you create for yourself, one that you and only you would ever "read" quite that way.

12. *Day toning* includes the conscious use of reading as a way to affect the way we see the world. Day toning can be understood more clearly by likening it to visual after-images. You are probably acquainted with the optical experiment in which you stare for an extended period at a red circle on a white card, then focus immediately on a pure white card with no shape on it. But . . . you *do* see a shape, a circle the same size as the one you were just staring at. The "ghost" image is an after-effect. Reading has its after-effects, too, and they become part of our world. The more powerful the reading experience, the slower the decay of the after-effects. Some last a lifetime—by actually changing us. Psychologists have done some interesting studies of *visual* afterimages in reading, but I don't know if anyone has ever claimed to have measured the *emotional* after-effects of reading (Crowder 59 et passim). Regardless, you don't have to be a psychologist to know that reading changes how you feel. It's obvious. What isn't obvious is why so few of us capitalize on it.

My grandmother, who is anything but an intellectual, has survived adversity partly by reading books that, in her words, "put my mind at ease and in tune with the infinite." No one taught her to do this. Every night, sometimes for hours, she immerses her mind in inspirational literature that ranges from "positive thinking" to Christian Science to semi-mystical meditation. Judged as literature, many of these texts are insignificant, but it is undeniable that they have a powerful effect on their readers. At a very advanced age, my grandmother is relatively optimistic, even-tempered, and strong of mind; she is sure that spirit and energy come from the books she reads. In fact, she consciously uses these books for that very purpose. When she wakes up in the morning, it is after an evening of peaceful reading followed by restful sleep; in a sense, the previous night's reading is the foundation of the new day. She reads not so much for information or entertainment as for spiritual nourishment, the way a monk or nun might read sacred texts. She proscribes and maintains the tone of her day by what she chooses to read.

It reminds me of when, at the age of 16, I read Marcus Aurelius. Each reading of it imbued me with calm and the ability to concentrate. It was as though the author's stoicism—the attempt "to triumph over the vicissitudes and alterations of life by maintaining a constant temper in the face of a changing world"—had gently risen from the pages and slipped into my spirit (Leites 51). Floating through the house, I even had a civil word for my parents. The effect soon wore off, in the face of a changing world, not to mention a changing self. At the same age, reading Kerouac's *On the Road*, I'd jump in the car, tune in Chuck Berry on the radio, and go, go, go.

Perhaps the younger we are, the more susceptible we are to what we read (or to what is read to us). Children can be made to cry by sad stories and to scream by scary ones. I remember being terrified by the story of the Three Billy Goats Gruff: I thought they would bite me or eat me. And I positively hated the troll. I didn't want to go to sleep that night.

Even now, what I read resonates throughout the day. While writing this book, I found myself alone in the country for a while. I went back and reread Alain Robbe-Grillet's novel *The Voyeur*. It's a strong little book. I admire it. But it left me feeling vaguely fearful and anxious, because fear and anxiety are two of its dominant moods. It made me worry about my dog's health, my son's future, my wife's safety, my book's progress, my mother's happiness, you name it! Fortunately, I was able to recognize the immediate source of my disquiet, and to apply an antidote to it by reading something equally strong but somewhat brighter in mood. I went straight to P. G. Wodehouse.

William Burroughs describes a slightly different type of day toning:

> For exercise, when I make a trip, such as from Tangier to Gibraltar, I will record this in three columns in a notebook I always take with me. One column will contain simply an account of the trip, what happened. I arrived at the air terminal, what was said by the clerks, what I overheard on the plane, what hotel I checked into. The next column presents my memories; that is, what I was thinking of at the time, the memories that were activated by my encounters; and the third column, which I call my reading column, gives quotations from any book that I take with me. . . . For example, I'm reading *The Wonderful Country* and the hero is just crossing the frontier into Mexico. Well, just at this point I come to the Spanish frontier, so I note that down in the margin. Or I'm on a boat or a train, and I'm reading *The Quiet American*. I look round and see if

there's a quiet American aboard. Sure enough, there's a quiet sort of young American with a crew-cut, drinking a bottle of beer. It's extraordinary, if you really keep your eyes open. I was reading Raymond Chandler, and one of his characters was an albino gunman. My God, if there wasn't an albino in the room. He wasn't a gunman. (Interview in *Paris Review* 28)

If day toning is affected by the content of what one reads, it is affected even more strongly (and subtly) by the quality of the material. Had *The Voyeur* been a shoddy piece of work, it would have been *really* depressing, perhaps even psychopathic. The fact that it is a work of art—well-conceived, original, and well-written—gave it a buoyancy that all good art has, no matter how negative the subject matter. What a horrible world Louis-Ferdinand Céline describes in *Death on the Installment Plan*, but how terrific it makes us feel to read that book! So the question is not always so much the material's content as it is the artfulness of the presentation. Just being in the general vicinity of great art makes us feel that life really is worthwhile.

People read for different reasons, and not everyone cares whether or not a book has literary greatness. The people who read romances probably want to forget themselves and to live vicariously. These readers judge a romance by how complete that vicarious experience is. And, without knowing it, they probably value a particular romance by how powerfully it radiates through them and onto their surroundings, so that for even just a moment the experiences and feelings in the book seem possible in the real world the reader lives in. (This willing suspension of disbelief is just a step away from sexual fantasy, which partly explains why sexual material has entered so easily into the romance genre.) Regardless of how sophisticated we are, this radiation—from text, to reader, to world—takes place any time we become involved with what we are reading.

It is odd that we do not make more conscious use of this power to transform our sense of ourselves and our surroundings. Is it because we're too busy reading what we think we *ought* to read? Do we waste too much time reading this or that novel because everyone is talking about it? (I almost never enjoy anything I've read for this reason.) Why don't we take the bull by the horns and read according to what we need? Have you been feeling trivial? Read some philosophy. Have you been stuck in the same town too long? Read about an exotic place. Has your imagination been running riot? Read a good how-to book on plumbing. Does your life seem too cut and dried? Go the the library, close your eyes, reach out and take a book, check it out, go home, and read every word of it. These are all creative *uses* of reading.

13. *Night toning.* Another creative use of reading involves manipulating the unconscious. I've already described how my grandmother used reading to induce calm into her sleeping mind. It reminds me of a suggestion made by poet Kenneth Koch. He said that if you want to have intense dreams about language, read Joyce's *Finnegans Wake* for several hours before bedtime, until you're really sleepy, so that when you put down the book you quickly fall asleep. He was right: I had "language" dreams all night.

One of the least creative—but creative nonetheless—uses of reading is as a soporific. How many millions of people keep a book on their bedside stand, reading only a few pages a night before conking out? It can't be that the book is so boring that they get drowsy, for in fact many bedside books are by favorite authors. No, there is something intrinsically soothing about the very act of reading, quietly, in bed late at night, free of intrusion. The nervous system, stimulated or irritated throughout the day, finally "unwinds." Then begins a silent conversation between author and reader, requiring a minimum of physical activity. The hands hold the book and from time to time turn the pages, the eyes move ever so slightly. It's as if, slowly but surely, the reader's body disappears, as it does in falling asleep. The mind is stimulated by an exciting book, but deep down it knows that at any time it can easily discontinue the excitement: it is in control of the situation. Also, it is being gratified and in some real sense nourished by the interaction between the book and itself, and, like the appetite that tells us we needn't eat another bite, the mind senses when it has had enough satisfaction. Like love and meaningful work, this satisfaction is fulfilling. It allows us to feel that, for the time being, all is well with the world. We fall asleep, not because we are bored, but because we are content. The whole process is only mildly creative, but, given the circumstances, perhaps mildness is exactly what is called for.

It would be wonderful to be able to read in one's sleep. I've done some reading in my dreams, usually of single poems that I'd "forgotten" I'd written. Every once in a great while, I'll dream that I'm reading some new or forgotten book, which turns out to be amazingly beautiful and revelatory. Interestingly, those people who are able to control their dreams, to have what are called "lucid" dreams, purport that they are unable to make words appear and then to read them. According to one lucid dreamer, the letters "just won't hold still" (LaBerge 102). Perhaps the brain cannot perform these two functions—create words and read them—simultaneously.[6] Perhaps this is why some of us have trouble with normal reading when we're awake: unknowingly, in our heads we create words that compete with the words on the page, and in some sense the words just won't hold still. The exercises in this chapter are designed to make you more aware of that process, to enable you to make the words fly away or hold still.

14. *Stencils.* In college, I became interested in filmmaking. I read books about directing, cinematography, lighting, and editing, and I started looking at movies differently. I began to notice how the camera framed each shot, how it zoomed in, pulled back, or panned, whether it was stationary or tracking, and whether the shot was a close-up, middle range, or distance one. It was particularly illuminating to focus my attention on anything other than what the filmmaker wanted the audience to focus on. If a close-up of an actress's face emphasized the dreamy look in her eyes, I'd study her earrings. If a violent bar fight were in progress, I'd examine the decor. From time to time, I'd shut my eyes for a few minutes, to make myself more aware of the background music. Or I'd look only at red objects, or at shoes, or at one corner of the screen.

I also started watching television analytically. To make it easier, I cut out various shapes of dark paper (such as construction paper) and placed them over the screen.

Let's say you have a television set whose screen is 11 inches wide by 8 inches tall. Cut out a dark rectangle 7 inches wide by 4 inches tall and place it on the middle of the screen. (The static electricity in the screen will probably hold the paper in place.) Now watch television for an hour or so. Afterward, ask yourself how the mask affected the way you watched. What did you notice for the first time? What did you see that you probably wouldn't have seen? How much of the program did you "miss" because you couldn't see something essential to understanding it? Do you think that in some ways the show looked better or more interesting?

Try other shapes—circles, oblongs, triangles, irregular shapes— and other sizes. Try combinations of shapes at various locations on the screen. Try taking sheets of paper the size of your screen and cutting shapes *out* of them, through which you can glimpse the programs. I've always been partial to looking through shapes, rather than around them (the screen as keyhole?).

Now apply the same procedure to reading. Take a piece of poster board (or heavy paper), cut out some shapes, place the board against the page, and read only what shows through the holes (Figure 17 a–d). Because book pages are usually smaller than television screens, the holes should be commensurately smaller.

You can read the same page at least eight different times with one stencil, by pointing it up, down, left, and right, and then by turning it over and again pointing it up, down, left, and right. Of course, you can point it in any direction you want, and, if you want to develop real

Figure 17a. Grid example.

Figure 17b.

Figure 17c.

Figure 17d.

panache at this technique, you can move the stencil as you read. Other ways of breaking up the usual left-to-right pattern are:

- reading diagonally, from top left to bottom right, beginning in the upper right-hand corner of each page, and moving down, as shown in Figure 18 ("New Slant").

- reading in a whirlpool pattern, beginning anywhere on the edge of the page and spiraling inward to the center, as shown in Figure 18 ("Père Ubu").

- reading each page's topic sentences first, then running your eye down the center of the page, as in Figure 18 ("Skeleton").

- reading as if along the frame of a picture, as in Figure 18 ("Border Patrol").

These are just four of many possible patterns.

15. *Sound Off.* At home I sometimes watch television with the sound off, inventing the music, sound effects, and dialogue, out loud or silently. Sometimes I try to make the music and dialogue match the picture, and sometimes I make them as divergent as possible, while still maintaining some coherence between them. The conscious mind always wants to make sense of things, to find a connection between seemingly disparate elements. As William Burroughs says:

> You take a television set, shut off the sound-track and put on any arbitrary sound-track and it will seem to fit. You show a bunch of people running for a bus in Picadilly and put in machine-gun sound effects and it will look like Petrograd in 1917; people will assume that they are running because they're being machine-gunned. (Odier 16)

Woody Allen used a similar technique in his film *What's Up, Tiger Lily?* He took an ordinary Japanese crime film and, without knowing Japanese, wrote subtitles for it. The original story was about a bunch of Japanese crooks fighting over a briefcase containing narcotics. In Woody Allen's version, these thugs are fighting over a suitcase containing a *recipe*. Thus, the comic premise is established, and the humor falls into place around it. I've often wondered why schools with video equipment don't have their students take an old film and dub in new dialogue. It's a simple technique from which students would learn a lot, and have a good time doing it.

You can do much the same with foreign language comic books and picture books, and with what are called in Spanish *fotonovellas*. (The *fotonovella* is a story told with photographs showing actors and actresses posed in actual locations.) In comic books and *fotonovellas*, the dialogue is presented in speech balloons, with narrative continuity ("The next day . . .") in little rectangles, often in the upper left-hand corner of the frame.

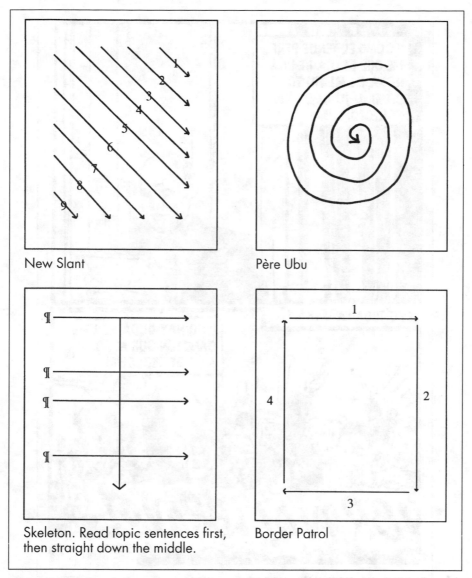

New Slant

Père Ubu

Skeleton. Read topic sentences first,
then straight down the middle.

Border Patrol

Figure 18. Four reading patterns.

(Figure 19 shows an example.) I know a little Spanish, so when I come to
a word or expression I don't know, I just make a wild guess and keep
reading. Such versions of the stories can be more interesting and enter-
taining than the originals.

If you get really ambitious and want to extend this form of reading
into writing, take some white tempera or White-Out and blank out all the

Figure 19. Spanish comic.

words. Then go back and write new ones. You might also want to cut out some of the boxes and rearrange them, as I did with artist Joe Brainard in *Cherry*, a comic strip work based on a *fotonovella*. (See Figure 20a–e.)

Watching films and television without the sound or reading comics without the words forces you to imagine, to create, to take an active part in the experience, the way listening to the radio did years ago.

Figure 20a. *Cherry* comic strip by Joe Brainard and Ron Padgett.

Figure 20b.

Figure 20c.

Figure 20d.

Figure 20e.

16. *Foreign languages.* It is highly challenging—some would say maddening—to try to make sense of words in an unfamiliar alphabet, such as Russian, and even more taxing to understand words written with an unfamiliar, non-alphabetic system, such as Chinese. With Russian and Chinese, I have some idea of where words begin and end, but not so with, say, Arabic, which to me looks like an uninterrupted flow of elegant curls, flips, and dots.

As long as my patience holds out, though, I like letting my eyes pass over the words of foreign languages. Sometimes I begin to notice patterns, repetitions of letters, letter combinations, or characters. Hawaiian, for instance, looks liquid and rounded, with lots of vowels and vowel digraphs. (A digraph is a combination of two or more vowels in which each vowel retains its distinct pronunciation. For example, the *oa* in "Samoa" is a digraph.) The entire Hawaiian language reminds me of the Hawaiian somatic type, rounded, smooth, and liquid, like the long waves that roll in from the Pacific.

A friend of mine improved his rudimentary Italian by a method that at first sounds simple-minded. He got some books in Italian, opened to the first page, and let his eyes go over the words until he got to the last page. Then he'd "read" another book. And so on. It was as though he were a child imitating adults by "play-reading." After a while he began to feel comfortable with certain patterns, and his vocabulary expanded naturally, because he saw new words over and over in various contexts.

When I first went to France, I knew some college French, but I neither spoke nor read French with ease. My reading in French had been limited to lyric poetry and short fiction; I never read long novels. Living on a student budget in (by then) expensive Paris, I found that I had little money for "entertainment." My solution was to buy hefty novels in cheap paperback editions and read for long hours into the evenings. These books contained new vocabulary, unfamiliar turns of phrase, and slang. My understanding was spotty and, in a technical sense, erroneous, because I tended to invent meanings for whatever was unfamiliar (see #15, *Sound Off*, above). Gradually, though, I began to understand new words and phrases, not by looking them up in the dictionary but by deducing their meanings from their contexts. I noticed that certain writers had "pet" words and phrases. But what I gained was something more fundamental than a larger vocabulary; I began to get a "feel" for the flow of the language, its syntactical structures, its tone. After some months of such reading, I found that I was no longer translating the French into English in my head (a form of subvocalization that not only slows us down but also distances us from the original text). I was reading "in" French.

At about that time, I also began to dream in French. In these dreams I spoke with astonishing fluency, and when I woke up, I had the strong impression that the French in the dream was not a phony, made-up French, but the real thing. In other words, when my conscious mind let go, I was able to speak more naturally.

This was certainly true after a few glasses of wine: I found myself taking part in spirited conversations in French. Unfortunately I don't recall reading French while tipsy. Perhaps it was like reading on "speed": all night you devour huge tomes with total understanding, but when you wake up late the following afternoon you can't remember all that much, and what remains most vivid is simply the exhilaration of the experience. Apparently, what we read in an "altered state" is stored in the short-term memory, where it quickly decays. Still, having a glass of wine is a good way to relax enough to let your eyes go over the words in, say, a Polish newspaper. When you go back to reading English, English seems so clear and easy.

When I say "English" I mean contemporary American. Contemporary *English* English is, of course, not the same as American English; Elizabethan English even less so, and so on, back to Middle English and Old English. Old English (or Anglo-Saxon) is virtually a foreign language. Try deciphering, for instance, the first passage below (from *The Song of Caedmon*, ca. A.D. 900):

> Nu [we] sculon herian   Heofon-rices Weard,
> Meotodes meahte   and His mod-zepanc,
> weorc Wuldor-Faeder,   swa He wundra zehwaes,
> oece Dryhten,   or onstealde.
> He aerest [ze] scop   ielda bearnum
> Heofon to hrofe,   haliz Scieppend;
> pa middan-zeard   mann-cynnes Weard,
> oece Dryhten   aefter teode —
> firum foldan   Frea eall-mihtiz.

(Bornstein 6)

Notice how much simpler and more "modern" is the next excerpt, from the early fourteenth century (the boldface **p** stands for Old English "thorn"):

> The bee has thre kyndis. Ane is, **p**at scho es never yfill, and scho es noghte with thaym **p**at will noghte wyrke, bot castys thaym owte and puttes thayme awaye. Anothire is, **p**at when scho flyes scho takes erthe in hyr fette, **p**at scho be noghte lyghtly overheghede in the ayere of wynde. The thyrde es, **p**at scho kepes clene and brychte hire wyngez. (Richard Rolle, in Bornstein 65)

When I refer to "foreign languages," the term can here be stretched to include forms of English other than standard: early English, dialects, and pidgin.

17. *Typing.* In the early 1960s, I learned that one of the best ways to read an author was to type up his or her work at some length. I had typed up brief selections from other people's work—individual poems or paragraphs, bits of dialogue, extracts from an essay—but it wasn't until I typed an entire collection of poems (the 66 poems in the first edition of Ted Berrigan's *Sonnets*) that I understood how close you can get to another's work by this means.

This procedure has several requirements. First, you must be able to type, obviously, but well enough so that it isn't just a big chore. Conversely, you can't be too good a typist, the kind that can breeze along without even reading the original material. Many of us fall somewhere between, perfect for this reading method.

Typing Ted's poems made me realize that their basic unit of construction was less the clause or phrase than single words placed side by side ("like bricks," as he put it). I also noticed that he favored words that had a weightiness, a physical presence. Words like "shackled," "frolicsome," "unabridged," and "Berrigan." This vocabulary gave the work a certain heft, which he kept from being burdensome by means of the light melody of vowels that played in and out. Using the carriage return, I was also able to focus more clearly on the way he used line breaks, and how these affected the momentum of the entire work.

Later, typing John Ashbery's poetry just so I could read it more closely, I noticed how his use of conjunctions lent the work a great forward motion. I don't think I would have noticed these (and other) characteristics had I not slowed my reading to a rate closer to that of the creation of the original, simulating the position of the author.

Choose a piece by a favorite writer. Type it up, at length. What do you notice that you hadn't noticed before?

Variant for the tough of mind: do the above with the work of a writer you dislike.

18. *Reading the blank page.* Many writers have described their anxiety at facing the blank sheet of paper, a feeling readers do not share because, obviously, readers face pages with words (which for some has its own anxiety). Most of these writers also say that once they get started writing, the anxiety vanishes and they get involved in the act of writing, which sometimes is pleasurable and exciting. By learning to read the blank page, readers can obtain a similar pleasure and excitement.

The method is simple. Get a bound volume with blank pages—there are various sizes available from stationers, art stores, and card shops. (For the purposes of a preliminary experiment, you could even use a printed book that has blank pages at the end.) Look at the top center of the first blank page, as if a title were there, and use as the title whatever pops into your head. Immediately move your eyes down and to the left, to where the text would start on a printed page, and move them from left to right, just as you would if you were reading, but all the time allowing that inner voice—the one that said the title to you—to keep talking. Allow it to say anything it wants. Continue to move your eyes at your normal reading pace, until you get to the bottom of the page. Then go on to the next page. What you're doing is a sophisticated variation on the play-reading of young children.

The first time I tried this method, I was surprised by how easy it was. I was sitting in my pickup truck in the parking lot of a supermarket at night, waiting for my wife. I lost interest in watching people get in and out of their cars, so I picked up the book on the seat next to me, a novel by Muriel Spark called *A Far Cry from Kensington*, and I read the first page, in which the main character, Mrs. Hawkins, says:

> You can set your mind to anything most of the time. You can sit
> peacefully in front of a blank television set, just watching nothing;
> and sooner or later you can make your own programme much bet-
> ter than the mass product. It's fun, you should try it sometime. (5)

This suggestion seemed perfectly reasonable to me, but I stopped reading because the light in the parking lot was dim. I flipped idly through the book until I got to the blank pages at the end. These reminded me of a blank television set. Staring at a blank page, I tried Mrs. Hawkins's suggestion, and I heard words inside my head.

When I tried to move my eyes in anything other than the normal pattern of reading (left to right and top to bottom), the words stopped or became garbled. But when I resumed the normal pattern, the words flowed inside me again. After the third and last blank page, I realized that this method had worked, but that I was unable to recall clearly the details of the first (blank) page. Now, when I want to recall everything, I tape record myself reading the blank pages aloud.

The initial experiments resulted in something akin to stream-of-consciousness, but the more I practice the method, the more control I have over the material, provided that I stick with the normal patterns of eye movement.

I should add that reading the blank page is not to everyone's taste, and that initial attempts tend to last only five *or* ten minutes. It helps to loosen up the word flow by preceding the experiment with a few minutes of what might be called "freetalking," in which you talk aloud to yourself for a period of minutes, saying anything that comes into your head, so long as you do not stop talking.

The act of reading the blank page reminds me of a book by the poet Aram Saroyan, published around 1970 by Kulchur Press. The "book" consisted of a ream of mimeograph paper with the author's name and copyright notice modestly rubber-stamped on the wrapping. The "book" baffled readers. (It also caused the publisher's distributor to discontinue their business relationship.)

One also wonders about the reception of a book published in France under the title of *Nihil: Rien* by "Estrennes," which consisted of 100 blank pages.[7] Could Saroyan's book be considered a fortuitous translation of it?

In quite a different context, Wolfgang Iser has discussed the energizing role of what he calls the "blank" in fiction. For him, the blank can have various functions, but in general, it can be described as any missing element that acts as a "propellant for the reader's imagination, making him supply what has been withheld," because "as blanks mark the suspension of connectability between textual segments, they simultaneously form a condition for the connection to be established" (*The Act of Reading* 194, 195). By not telling everything, a work of fiction allows the reader to imagine the missing elements, to participate more actively in the creation of that which arises between text and engaged reader. Works with as few blanks as possible, such as propaganda fiction, attempt to control the reader's mind, not to activate it.

Iser presents a brief history of the novel in terms of how it has stimulated the reader to what he calls "acts of constitution." The eighteenth century saw the development of the fictitious reader—in effect a character, to whom the book is addressed—so that, as in Sterne's *Tristram Shandy*, the reader is subjected to the shifting perspectives of the narrator and the characters, while modulating his or her own responses so that those responses more or less match up with those expected of the fictitious reader (*The Implied Reader* 101–20). Things became more complex in the nineteenth century, when the narrator split off from the author, becoming, in effect, another character, whose point of view was no longer reliable. The number of blanks in the text increased in the twentieth century, culminating in Joyce's *Ulysses,* with its

> whole panoply of narrative techniques that the novel has evolved during its comparatively short history. But they are organized in an extraordinary way. They continually intersect, and this fragmentation makes it impossible to find a point at which they might converge or from which they might be guided. (Iser, *The Act of Reading* 207)

This disorientation—this onslaught of blanks—makes greater demands on the reader's ability to put it all together, to constitute the whole work.

What might the next step be in this history? Perhaps one in which the reader takes an even more active role, finally gaining the upper hand over the author. That is partly what I mean by creative reading.

7 Other Voices

Reading should come in different flavors.

—Gary Moore

By the age of five or six, most children have witnessed oral and silent reading. They have been read to (or seen people reading aloud) and they have seen others absorbed in silent reading. In school, oral and silent reading are confirmed as the two basic modes.

I remember my classmates reading aloud, stumbling over hard words and skipping small ones, their voices toneless or constricted, as the rest of us followed the text with our eyes. I remember their reading the words differently than I would have, and how uncomfortable their ineptitude made me feel. This procedure of one student reading aloud as the others follow silently is now considered pedagogically unsound: it induces a herky-jerky, regressive pattern in the eye movements, the very opposite of what the reading teacher is trying to inculcate. Likewise, choral reading is not so popular as it was; it causes students to read in a lumbering, singsong mass that distracts everyone from the text. In many classes, individual students read aloud to their classmates, who simply listen and do not follow the text silently with their eyes.

Oral reading relates the students' speaking vocabulary to their reading vocabulary; it develops their ability to differentiate between tones and to project those differences; it lends color and body—a physical presence—to the text. Oral reading also makes it possible for students to begin to listen to themselves. These are a few of the many good reasons for reading aloud.

Silent reading is trickier: it isn't always silent. In the first place, some people "move their lips," even going so far as to whisper the words. When I was a child, lip moving was associated with the way old people read; perhaps they read that way because they had never been told not to. My grandfather used to sit in his easy chair, reading the newspaper, unaware that a steady stream of subtle hissing was issuing from his lips (in whispering, the *s*'s always carry best).

But just as we were forbidden to count on our fingers, we were forbidden to move our lips during reading, mainly because the physical motion limits our speed. We can't say words as quickly as we can see them, and there's the added possibility that we might stumble over words simply because we don't know how to pronounce them correctly. Pure sight readers are often able to read and understand many words they've never said or heard, including words that can't be "sounded out" phonetically.

A more subtle and interesting aspect of silent reading occurs when readers keep their lips still, but "hear" in their heads the words on the page. This silent hearing is called "subvocalization." Reading teachers are now taught to discourage both lip moving and subvocalization. (My teachers never even brought up the idea of subvocalization.) Like lip moving, subvocalization is frowned upon because it reduces reading speed: you can't hear words as quickly as you can see them.

But, may I ask, what's the hurry? I *like* subvocalization. The books I most enjoy reading are those that have a definite "voice," a voice provided by the author. What this means is that the style is so distinct that we're able to communicate with a specific, real person: the author.

The author does this by writing either in the first person or the third person, as in these examples:

> I woke up around 7 and lay in bed thinking about getting up. After about an hour I did finally manage to swing my feet over the side of the bed and to place them flat on the cold marble floor.

> He woke up around 7 and lay in bed thinking about getting up. After about an hour he did finally manage to swing his feet over the side of the bed and to place them flat on the cold marble floor.

The difference in wording—a few changes of pronouns—is very slight, but its effect on the tone is larger. The two examples "feel" different from one another.

Some types of books lend themselves readily to either first- or third-person treatment. Autobiographies and nonfiction travel books are two of the simplest, most direct uses of the first person. (Gertrude Stein, always exceptional, wrote somebody else's autobiography: *The Autobiography of Alice B. Toklas.*) But, as we saw in the previous chapter, the first person is not always so cut and dried. In fiction, for instance, the "I" may not be the author; it might be a character created by the author to tell the story: the *narrator*. Although we usually assume a bond of trust between the author and us, we cannot make such an assumption between the narrator and us. Sometimes the narrator tells the story in a self-serving way, or simply lies. And what if the narrator turns out to be a lunatic? We cannot blame the author for the mental or moral condition of the narrator, any more than we can blame any other character for such conditions.

The voice in third-person writing is less thorny. Here it may be assumed to be that of the author, with no tricky intermediary. However, the voice can have great range, from the statistical report that is highly objective to the novel whose author is so engaged in the story that he or she cannot resist interrupting it to comment, praise, or blame.

Although most books are cast in essentially either one mode or the other, some have internal variations. Nonfiction in the third person often is interspersed with quotations in the first person. Some first-person novels might be more aptly called first-people novels: different chapters are narrated by different characters. Such novels often use those characters' names as the chapter title ("Chapter 1: Bill. Chapter 2: Frederika"). In both these variations, though, the reader knows at all times who is speaking.

This does not hold true for certain modern works. In Joyce's *Finnegans Wake,* we are hard pressed to say who is speaking. Is it the author? A character? Or characters? The same goes for Eliot's "Waste Land," Ashbery's poem "The Skaters," or Ted Berrigan's *Sonnets.* In a burst of immodesty, I'll add my own work to this group, a novel called *Antlers in the Treetops,* written in collaboration with Tom Veitch. The voice in *Antlers* shifts every few paragraphs, from author(s), to one character, then another, then to an entirely different author or set of authors, requiring the reader to invent a new voice every few paragraphs.

For, if we become involved with a text, we tend to invent a voice to hear it in. We invent what we assume is an appropriate tone of voice, such as the laconic, manly voice of Hemingway in the Nick Adams stories, the exquisite, sometimes peevish voice of Sei Shonagon in her *Pillow Book,* the sophisticated, subtly modulated voice of Henry James in *The Golden Bowl,* the robust voice of Whitman in *Leaves of Grass,* the angular and deceptively quiet voice of Emily Dickinson in her poems. Sometimes when I read such authors, I "hear" these voices quite clearly. This subvocalization has a bonding effect on me and the words. That it causes me to read slower is anything but a drawback, it is exactly what I want! I love the feeling that the author is speaking to me, as if he or she were in the room with me. This is particularly exciting if the author lived far away and long ago.

Inventing these voices can be, I admit, shaky business. If you misinterpret the material, you intensify the error by inventing a voice based on the misinterpretation. Inventing the voices of writers from other cultures can be particularly risky. For some, the temptation, when reading Chinese poetry, might be to "hear" it as if its authors were essentially one big lyrical Charlie Chan; that is, our cultural stereotypes can force widely different works into one mold. In doing so, we take the work one step farther away from the original, just as the translation into English did, and the farther away we get from the origin, the less of its character remains.

Work that has little character in the first place is immune to such misinterpretation. Dry, official, toneless writing is dry, official, and toneless in translation, and it has the same "voice" as that which issues from the mouths of so many public and private officials. These people speak unnaturally because their speech imitates, and rather poorly, at that, formal, written language. When our education does not succeed in teaching us to think in complex structures, we cannot speak in complex structures either. We cannot utter long, grammatically complex (and correct) sentences; we cannot arrange our thoughts into logical groups; and we cannot order such groups into a cohesive whole. To compensate, we use technical and official jargon, fashionable "buzz" words, and important-sounding latinisms. Alas, such a way of speaking precipitates into the culture, like acid rain. Inventing accurate voices for the texts written by such people can hardly be called invention; it is, rather, an exercise in memory. In public, the speaker talks like bad writing, thinks like bad writing, and in private creates more bad writing; the reader immediately recognizes this universal voice, so unmistakable on the page. The whole chain of thinking, writing, and reading not only has no originality, but also has no connection with the natural voice (in both senses of the word). If only some of these people who make speeches and give news conferences would talk to us the way they talk (we assume) at home! If we cannot have clear public speech of intellectual character, let us have at least a little down-home authenticity.

But we have little of that. So what are we to do with such dull material? Well, we can simply not read it.

Or we can try *voice substitution*. It's an old technique used by comedians, but never, so far as I know, applied to reading. All you have to do is substitute a "voice" different from that of the text. For example, when reading the text of a dictator, imagine it being delivered by Donald Duck. If the text of a "tobacco industry spokesman" bores you, imagine it in the voice of a professional wrestler. If you are driven up the wall by the platitudes of a school commencement address, imagine it being delivered in the voice of Marlene Dietrich or Hattie McDaniel.

This is similar to a method used by comic musician Spike Jones. The typical Spike Jones song begins with soothing, romantic material, as in "Cocktails for Two":

> Oh what delight to
> Be given the right to

> Be carefree and gay once again,
> No longer slinking
> Respectably drinking
> Like civilized ladies and men,
> No longer need we miss
> A charming scene like this:
> In some secluded rendez-vous. . . .

Suddenly a maniacal voice shrieks "Whoopee!," a police whistle sounds, a gun fires, and the music goes completely wild. The vocalist maintains his suavity, but is constantly undercut with burlesque sound effects (his crooning of "And we'll enjoy a cigarette" is followed by an emphysemic cough). This undercutting radically transforms the original material. It's a shame more young people don't know about Spike Jones; he is a delightful way to learn about broad parody and burlesque.

Jones was the master of his style, but his range was narrow. You might want to try more subtle transformations. In any case, combine whatever voice with whatever material you wish, keeping in mind that the greater the difference between voice and text, the more bizarre (and sometimes comic) the effect.

A similar set of techniques can be applied to reading good writing. Let's say you are hooked on the crime novels of Elmore Leonard. Let's also say you have a favorite uncle who used to run numbers. Why not imagine his voice reading Elmore Leonard to you? That's what the companies that produce spoken arts records do: they try to match up the voice with the material. They paired off Irish actress Siobhan McKenna and James Joyce's writing; they hired Jay Silverheels (who played Tonto in the Lone Ranger radio programs and movies) to read Native American poems and tales; they got spooky Vincent Price to read the horror tales of Edgar Allan Poe. You can use anyone's voice—a famous person's or a friend's—as the "voice" of the book.

When, after many attempts, I finally broke the Proust barrier and got so far into *Remembrance of Things Past* that I never wanted to get out, I found that the book provided its own voice for me to hear, the voice of Marcel, the narrator. It was a cultured, sensitive voice. One afternoon a friend came by for a nice, long chat. That night, when I resumed my reading, I heard *his* voice instead of Marcel's, as I recorded in a poem:

Reading Proust
I am aware of the volume,
the pages, their size and color

and their texture, with edges
and their words set in blocks
surrounded with margins,
And I am aware too of the meaning
of the words and sentences,
the majestic flotilla of the paragraphs
in the flow of the story—I recognize
the characters and remember them
from page to page, and I note
the art of the writing and the quality
of the author's mind, and I see him
writing his book, the words of which
I hear being read aloud to me
by a friend, whom I saw today
and who had stayed in my mind,
offering, while there, to perform
this service.

Literal oil flowed across

Then I went on reading

(Padgett, *Tulsa Kid* 28)

Given my friend's personality, the substitution worked fine. My friend became "Marcel" for that night. The next day, I went back to using the original Marcel voice, refreshed by the respite from it.

The experience of hearing a friend's voice in my head was more frequent when I was in my early twenties. In those days I would often spend 10 or 12 hours with Ted Berrigan, the poet, who was a Rabelaisian conversationalist with a highly distinct way of talking. Each time we parted, his voice continued to reverberate in my head. Everything I read I heard in his voice. Everything I said sounded as if he were saying it. Of course, the remembered voice "decayed" over the next few days, and I returned to a more various way of hearing. (Every time I see the word *various,* though, I hear a little of Frank O'Hara, who used the word *variously* so beautifully in one of his poems, and of Lionel Trilling, who used it frequently in his lectures.) People who are young enough to be impressionable but old enough to do good imitations are prime candidates for learning how to assimilate voices, store them, and use them in their reading. It also helps, of course, to live in a culturally diverse society, although I suppose that anyone with a television set has access to a wide variety of voices.

We should not overlook the possibility of applying *incongruous* voices to good writing. When the poetry of Wallace Stevens starts to sound overintellectualized, I sometimes "hear" it in the voice of a Southern redneck. T. S. Eliot's poetry is particularly delightful when heard in a strong Oklahoma accent ("Aprul eh-is thuh croolist munth"). I like to imagine how William Carlos Williams' poems—so American—would sound in an Italian accent. I would like to be able to "hear" an Eskimo cast perform *A Midsummer Night's Dream,* a Jamaican read *Paradise Lost.* We can also combine authors in any number of ways; we can, for instance, imagine T. S. Eliot in the unforgettable voice of Truman Capote, or vice versa. Such unusual pairings result in what amounts to burlesque, but frequently in the burlesque you see clearly an aspect of the writer's work that was previously too familiar to be noticed. The forest and the trees are separated.

Our own voices are the most familiar of all. That is to say, when we speak we are so accustomed to hearing ourselves that we cease to notice how we sound, unless there are unusual circumstances, such as a "frog in the throat" or a tape recording. Most people, hearing themselves on tape for the first time, ask, "Is *that* me? Do I really sound like that?" The reason the voice on the tape sounds different is that we are receiving the sound waves solely from outside our heads, whereas when we speak, we hear the sound from both inside and outside our heads. The new experience of hearing ourselves only from the outside makes most of us feel that we sound horrible, partly because we are distressed to find that we aren't what we had always thought we were, partly because we become self-conscious when attention—like a camera—is directed on us.

In learning to read better and more creatively, however, attention to self is exactly what is called for. You might ask yourself:

- Do I subvocalize?
- Do I subvocalize sometimes or always? Does the subvocalized voice flicker in and out?
- Do I subvocalize when it isn't necessary (as in reading the contents listing on a food can)?
- Do I subvocalize in different voices? If so, how do I arrive at those voices?
- Do I subvocalize in only one voice? What or whose voice is it?

Many people use a combination of the above. They don't subvocalize single words (like STOP on a street sign) or brief phrases; nor do they subvocalize certain types of material, such as scientific and mathematical data, lists of facts, flat nonfiction, and the like. They do subvocalize some poetry (where the sound can be crucial to the whole experience of the work) and fiction (they might "hear" British novels in an English accent, for instance). But, by and large, the single most common voice used in subvocalization seems to be a ghost version of one's own speaking voice. This voice is the old reliable of voices, the one that arises naturally when needed, when no other voices suggest themselves. (It is also the one we hear when we think in words.) So in a sense, when we use our own voice for subvocalization, we are not simply reading to ourselves, we are appropriating the text, modeling it to our own tone, reshaping its emotional contours. Without changing the words, we are rewriting the text.

This discussion of voice in reading would be incomplete without mention of a relatively recent phenomenon: the availability of the author's actual voice. In the past 40 years, there has been a tremendous increase in the number of live performances and recordings by authors reading their own work.

Before the 1950s, relatively few American authors read their work to large groups in public; only one poet comes readily to mind: Vachel Lindsay. Coffeehouse poetry readings were not uncommon in Greenwich Village and the Lower East Side of New York in the 1920s and 1930s, but their audiences were small and localized. Most of the poetry readings in the 1940s and early 1950s were by "distinguished" older poets—mostly men, although Gertrude Stein was an exception—who were invited to read their poetry or perhaps deliver a talk at a university. The big breakthrough occurred when Dylan Thomas toured America. Thomas's musical and dramatic intonations swept listeners off their feet; you can get some idea of the distinctive power of his voice by listening to any of the recordings still readily available. I remember hearing his recording of "Fern Hill" when I was in high school. I had read the poem before, but I wasn't prepared for the great lyrical blast of his voice. It sent me back to the printed page, and when I got there and silently read the poem again, I could hear his voice "singing" it to me. To this day I subvocalize Dylan Thomas's voice when reading his work.

His voice is congruent with his work, as is Wallace Stevens's, Edna St. Vincent Millay's, Allen Ginsberg's, and those of many others. Other voices come as surprises. I read John Ashbery's early work for several years before hearing him read, and I subvocalized a voice for it, a voice something like John Wayne's. Ashbery's real voice came as a shock. It seemed—partly as a result of my expectations—rather nasal. Later I adjusted to his voice, which after all was not so bad, and which blended perfectly with his new work, "perfectly" because in fact I was unable to read it without hearing his voice.

Did I understand his work any better, then? Some might argue that my original fantasy (the John Wayne voice) was, in fact, a more accurate representation of what has been called Ashbery's status as an "executive" poet. Is there always an advantage—or any advantage—in being acquainted with the author's speaking voice?

After listening to hundreds and hundreds of writers read their work, I've come to the conclusion that in some cases it helps, in some cases it doesn't. Some good writers read their own work poorly, making you wish you had stayed home with your own fantasy of the voice. Some writers who seem good read their work in such a way that you realize, hearing them, that their work isn't very good after all; its faults are revealed by the glare of public presentation. Other writers, whose work sometimes seems difficult on the page, come through with perfect clarity when they read it aloud. Here I'm thinking particularly of poets Kenneth Koch and Edwin Denby. Koch's gentle irony is perfectly clear and appropriate, as are Denby's shifting tones of everyday speech. When one goes back to their work on the page, the writing remains forever clarified. When hearing an author read, though, it's important to keep in mind that reading styles change, just as literary styles do. We shouldn't be disconcerted, for example, by the "old-fashioned" voice of "modernist" Ezra Pound.

The great opportunity we as readers have—with multitudes of public readings, tapes, and records now available—is to be able to invite not only an author's work into our minds, but his or her voice as well. We have the opportunity of measuring the author's voice against whatever voice we had created for that author, and from there, of pondering the relative qualities of both. From this we move toward a greater understanding of what the work is (or isn't).

Here are some other ways to experiment with reading aloud:

1. *Duets:* one person reads silently while another person reads a different text aloud. What effect does this have on the silent reader? How does the selection of material change the effect? Alternative: have both read different texts aloud.

2. *Choral readings:* a large group of people—a classroom-full, for instance—simultaneously read different texts, creating a sort of sound environment. This can be orchestrated, to make it resemble the general hum of conversation in a restaurant, theater, or sports arena; to make it harmonious (as in a round such as "Row, Row, Row Your Boat"); to make it euphonious (perhaps creating an abstraction using a text with similar vowel and/or consonant sounds); to make it chaotic, with everyone reading completely different texts, either whispered or shouted.

A variation of choral reading is to have a group read in unison a text that is identical except for, say, its nouns. (Such a text can easily be prepared by having each person fill-in-the-blanks.) What effect does such a reading have on the feel of the text? This exercise is not unlike the singing of "Happy Birthday to You," when everyone is in unison except when it comes to the name of the birthday person, who, it often turns out, is called by several different names. When the group momentarily divides at that point, the song always gets a little shaky.

Another option is to create word environments. Have the group simultaneously read aloud words that suggest:

- the ocean (*water, waves, whitecaps, splash, glug, crash, shhhh, whoosh,* etc.)
- the desert (*sand, palm tree, hot, dry, lizard, thirsty, sun, gasp,* etc.)
- night (*cool, dark, quiet, crickets, moon, stars, sleep,* etc.)
- the woods (*trees, green, wind, leaves, crunch, quiet, buzz, calm, alone,* etc.)

A variation of these word scenes is to combine words and sounds, as in:

- an orchestra, in which the *sounds* of the instruments are supported by a *basso continuo* of sentences of words *about* music
- a barnyard or zoo, in which animal sounds are mixed with words about animals
- a factory, with whistles, chugs, booms, and clicks mixed with words about manufacturing.

These exercises are fun in themselves, but they also set us to thinking about how to read aloud material that might be considered unreadable. How, for instance, would you read aloud what the man is saying in Figure 21?

Figure 21. Cussing man.

The picture of the cussing man is a clue that makes the typographical symbols (in the speech balloon) into international symbols. Readers in Martinique or the Philippines or Albania would be able to "read" what he is saying.

How would you read the semicolon in Ron Loewinsohn's poem (Figure 22)? Obviously, the poet has created this poem more as a treat for the eye than for the ear, which is partly why it's challenging to try to figure out a good way to read it aloud.

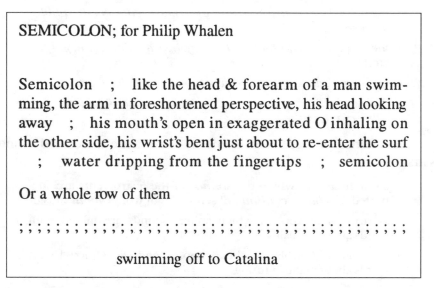

Figure 22. Ron Loewinsohn poem.

Take a look at the poem in Figure 23, by Paul de Vree. At first, it looks like a bunch of random letters and parentheses thrown up into the air, but if you look at it for a moment you'll notice that the letters are those of the title of a famous song, with something else thrown in. How would you read this poem aloud? I think I'd have four or five friends read it with me. I'd have everyone read or sing the words, out of synch, and perhaps with fluttery voices, since the parentheses remind me of birds fluttering around in the airy springtime Paris sky.

Another exercise is called *megaphone*. As you read any text aloud, get louder and louder, then softer and softer, then louder again, then softer again, and so on. Read so the change in volume has nothing to do with the text's content.

There are several variations on *megaphone*, based on pitch. As you read aloud, start with your voice pitched low and have it gradually go up

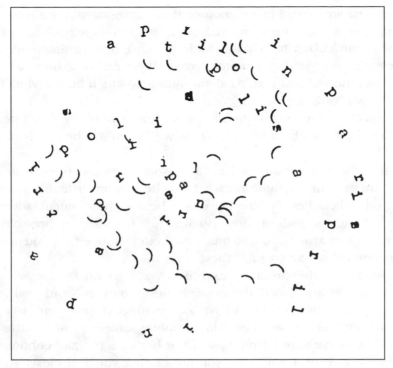

Figure 23. Paul de Vree poem.

as high as it can; then back down, and so on. Or have a pitch "twist" on each word, so that the voice rises on each word:

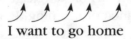

I want to go home

or falls on each:

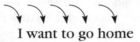

I want to go home

or alternates, one word with a rising twist, the next with a falling:

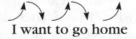

I want to go home

or with no change at all—a monotone:

I want to go home.

It's easier to read in a monotone if you imagine you're a robot or if you simulate a computer-generated voice. Intentionally reading in a monotone is particularly helpful for children whose oral reading tends to be toneless; the exaggerated monotone makes them realize that there is such a thing as tone and that reading aloud sounds so much better when it has tone, the way ordinary speech does.

Another voice skill valuable for reading is totally silent: listening. Listening is a form of reading, insofar as we "listen" to the words of what we read.

Try the following exercise. Close your eyes and open your ears: that is, focus your attention on what you hear. Keep listening until you think you've heard everything there is to hear at the moment, sounds in the far distance, sounds up close (such as that of your own breathing). If there are voices around you, so much the better. Notice how you immediately become more aware of all these sounds.

Here's another listening exercise. Ask a friend to talk with you while your eyes are closed. Pay close attention to every word your friend says, not just to the gist of them. Notice the tone, volume, and pace, and check to see if the words come in complete sentences or in little fragments. Then have your friend close his or her eyes too and continue the conversation. After a while, do you notice that you feel closer to your friend? Such a feeling of closeness occurs whenever we really listen to the other person, undistracted by other sounds, including those of our own thoughts. We interlock with our friend's words, and, in that sense, we show respect. We show that we feel that our friend's words are worthy of close attention.

Reading teachers, especially those in "whole language" classrooms, have become more aware of the importance of listening. Discussing the reading abilities of the deaf and the blind, Jeanne Chall says:

> Common sense tells us that the deaf would be the better readers because they can see the print. Yet the blind are the better readers. This happens because reading is closer to hearing than to seeing. (*Stages* 128)

Good teachers consider listening an active skill that must be practiced and developed, especially in light of the passive hearing most children grow up with, sitting in front of the television, which, after all, is primarily a visual medium, one whose words (and music) are often not worth listening to anyway. But even those who grow up without television need to maintain their listening power, to overcome their natural tendency toward aural numbness. And if one wants to read more creatively, the ability to listen carefully and continuously is even more crucial.

Finally, here are two exercises, for one person.

1. Pick any book and alternate reading silently and orally from it, alternating words, phrases, or sentences (the larger the syntactical unit, the easier the exercise).

2. How slowly can you read aloud and still retain the meaning of a sentence? Try reading any text aloud, slower and slower, until you're saying it word by word. After you say a word, keep your eyes on it; don't peek ahead to the next one. When you've really slowed down to, say, one word per 10 seconds, notice what your mind does in the silent intervals.

After doing any of the exercises in this chapter, you'll find that your normal reading has become smoother, easier, and clearer.

8 New Reading

The twentieth century has changed the way we read, and the change has been relatively abrupt. The proliferation of advertising, the "explosion" of the media, and the influence of modernism in literature have caused us to perceive words in ways foreign to our ancestors. By this I don't mean to trot out the old "what would Aristotle think if he saw computer graphics" type of truism. I mean to suggest that the change goes deeper, that our fundamental sense of what reading is and how to do it has changed.

Imagine that you are driving down a highway and you see, over on the right, the word "GAS" *six hundred miles* tall. The letters rest lightly on the ground, from where they sweep up through the clouds, their tops disappearing beyond the stratosphere. You would be astonished, like a hillbilly in the 1930s seeing a billboard for the first time. Until then the only words he might have ever seen—perhaps in the Bible—were tiny.

But you are sophisticated. You have seen faces 50 feet tall, moving and talking, as real as life. You are not like 91-year-old Harold Clough who, at his first movie as a boy in rural Vermont around 1912, saw a train heading toward him and got up and ran for his life. You have seen words written in vapor across the sky, you have seen them flow around the tops of buildings like a revolving halo, you have seen them fly toward you in different colors and explode (on TV and in computer games). You've seen them flash on and off, buck like a horse, and spell themselves out in neon script. You've seen them in a hundred different typefaces, big, fat, skinny, curly, leaning, antique, shadowed. You may have seen them deployed in fascinating new ways, combined with sound and images, in CD-ROMs.[1] Many of us have experienced these new presentations of words, which might be called the popular side of creative reading. Most of these forms are now so ordinary that we take them for granted.

Less common are the new ways of reading necessitated by modern literature. In 1897, when Stéphane Mallarmé's poem "A Throw of the Dice" was published, the literary page was given a new look: the lines, set in various sizes, were scattered around the page, so that the white space around the words suddenly took on an importance of its own. The poem even called into question whether or not we were to read it one page at a time or across the two-page spread. Christian Morgenstern's poem "Night Song" used symbols instead of alphabetical letters: it didn't need to be translated from the original German. The shaped poetry of the past—in which a poem had the physical shape of its subject matter—experienced a rejuvenation in the hands of Guillaume Apollinaire (see his poem "It's Raining" in Figure 24) and helped spawn what became known as "concrete poetry." The Italian Futurist poets espoused a kind of writing they called *parole in libertà*, or "words set loose" (Figure 25); words, sometimes truncated or dislocated, appeared in Cubist collages and paintings. In Switzerland, Germany, and France, the Dada poets experimented with chance poetry and sound poetry, as did Kurt Schwitters, the inventor of a one-man art movement, Merz. Apollinaire and Blaise Cendrars brought "found" elements into their poetry, such as the overheard chit-chat in the former's conversation-poem "Monday Rue Christine" and the latter's wonderful plagiarizations in his *Nineteen Elastic Poems* and *Documentaries*. Both poets were also attracted to advertising:

> You read the handbills the catalogs the posters that really
>   sing
> That's poetry and there are newspapers if you want prose
>   this morning[2]

Gertrude Stein's experimental repetitions made her prose pieces sound like delirious children's stories. Poets such as e. e. cummings took words apart and put them back together in unusual configurations. James Joyce, in *Finnegans Wake*, let the words run on in a kind of cosmic babble.

Obviously, modern literature has caused us to read in new ways.[3] But older literature does too. It all depends on what we mean by "new." Is it new as in "new to humankind" or new as in "new to me"? For example, is reading e. e. cummings for the first time really any more "new" than reading Chaucer (in Middle English) for the first time? The main difference between reading contemporary literature and reading classical literature is that the latter has a large body of criticism surrounding it, from which we can learn how other people have read it. Contemporary literature has fewer such "support systems." In deciding how to read a piece of writing that is radically new, we have to rely on our own nerve, gut reaction, and sense of what is beautiful and valuable. The more flexible we are in our reading, the more likely we are to be able to "handle" new work. If our literature is to be various and bold, flexibility in the way we read is crucial, because ultimately it is we who decide whether a work becomes part of our literature or just another forgotten book.

Finally, modern experimental literature has not only made us aware that there are many ways to read, but it has also intensified the traditional

IT'S RAINING

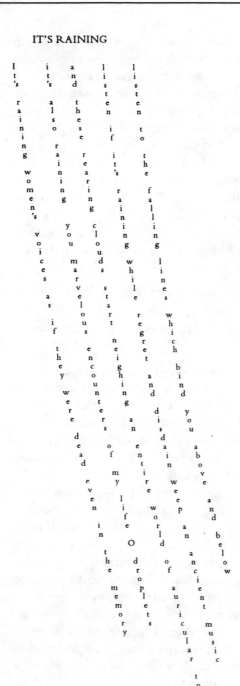

Figure 24. Apollinaire's "It's Raining" calligram.

Figure 25. Marinetti's "Parole in libertà."

intimacy of simply reading a book, spending time alone with an author in a quiet corner. As third grader Namah McKay put it:[4]

> **Myself!**
> I love to read,
> in a chair,
> in a bed,
> in a warm blanket,
> in front of a fire.
> My head is like a library,
> with many words and pages.
> I like the quietness,
> I like the quietness like a gentle breeze,
> I am like a lake,
> with boats of books
> crossing over me.

9 Reading in Unusual Situations

Sometimes people read in unusual situations and for different reasons in each of them. Poet C. K. Williams has written memorable poems about such situations, such as one about the guy who, starting to change a tire on a miserably cold January night, starts reading a page of an old newspaper he finds in the trunk (53).

Some people are able to read in cars or on trains, without motion sickness. Books such as *On the Road* might best be read in a car roaring down the highway. I found it extremely pleasant to ride in a small train across Sicily while comparing every bend in the track with its precise description in a guidebook:

> Again the track crosses Gaggera Stream, suddenly entering a long tunnel under Segesta Hill, and describes two long bends to the north, gaining elevation. After four other short tunnels (at 94 kilometers), Segesta Temple Station (elev. 243 m), 1.5 km north of the ruins.
> (Touring Club Italiano, 222–23, my translation)

Sometimes when I couldn't understand a sentence, I'd just look out the window and *see* what was being described. At these moments it was as if the reader's vision of the text, normally internal, had suddenly gone external. There was a delightful interplay between outside, text, and inside.

I took advantage of a trip to Martinique to reread Aimé Césaire's long poem *Notebook of a Return to the Native Land* (the land being Martinique). Originally I had found its language too rich and violent, but when I drove through the Martiniquin rain forest—the first I had ever seen, with its monstrous trees, huge flowers, and dense lushness—that leads up to Mont Pélé, the volcano that once sent a wave of lava over the island's largest town, killing its inhabitants in a few minutes, Césaire's explosive lushness seemed not only appropriate, but normal:

> I would rediscover the secret of great communications and great combustions. I would say storm. I would say river. I would say tornado. I would say leaf. I would say tree. I would be drenched by all rains, moistened by all dews. I would roll like frenetic blood on the slow current of the eye of words turned into mad horses into fresh children into clots into curfew into vestiges of temples into precious stones remote enough to discourage miners. Whoever would not understand me would not understand any better the roaring of a tiger. (43–45)

In the context of its natural setting, the poem seemed far less "exotic," and I felt, perhaps in a moment of self-delusion, that I was closer to the center of the poem, closer to feeling what it might have been like to have been the young Aimé Césaire writing it in the late 1930s. (It doesn't matter that he wrote it in France.) This type of reading helps us to be more where we are, or rather, to be there more fully.

Other times, we read to be elsewhere. The worst "escapist literature" (with sarcastic emphasis on "literature") is churned out for readers who want to identify with glamorous characters leading romantic and adventurous lives. I don't see anything wrong with a little escapism. It depends on what you're escaping from. If you're running from your personal problems, escapism is perhaps not such a good idea. If, on the other hand, you're fleeing an unpleasant reality over which you have no control, escapism seems pretty healthy to me. For instance, if you ride the subway to work in New York City every day, you eventually might read to block out the surroundings; it is far better to be on the dark parapet of a castle on the windy moor, than in a noisy, crammed, airless subway car. In such cases, reading to be somewhere else is eminently sane. And if you can escape to England with Barbara Pym or to Detroit with Elmore Leonard, so much the better. Besides, "being somewhere else" is at least as much emotional as it is temporal or geographical.

Where, mentally, are the people who, in big cities, read as they walk down the street? They walk slowly and they read slowly, glancing up from time to time to confirm their peripheral vision. The rest of us give them wide berth, as if they are blind. They take advantage of waiting at stop lights, and if deeply engrossed, they stand on the corner as the light changes from red to green to red to green. They have plenty of time. They are enclosed in the privacy of their own world. It is as though they are at home, taking a nice, long, leisurely bath. Seeing people reading as they walk has a soothing effect on others, because what is being read is more important at that moment than the outside world. It is a public declaration of faith in the inner life, just as strolling slowly in conversation with a good friend is a public declaration of the value of friendship.

Reading while strolling is a distinctly urban pleasure. I find it hard to imagine anyone reading while walking through the woods, along a mountain trail, or across a desert or ice floe: nature is inhospitable to ambulatory reading.[1] The same may be said for certain cities, especially the old parts of towns that have twisting streets, narrow sidewalks, and cobblestone paving. Only cities with streets in grid patterns, generous sidewalks, and moderate pedestrian traffic allow for reading while strolling.

On the other hand, nature can provide extraordinary situations for reading, if one stops and sits down, on a rock, log, a bed of dry leaves or pine needles, or, most comfortable of all, a mossy patch in sunlight. The timelessness of nature makes it easy to fall into the timelessness of the book, which is one of the reasons city dwellers like to read in the park. Natural settings form a precinct free from the pressures of "getting and spending" (as Edwin Denby put it) in which one always has to know what time it is. Reading *Walden* alone in the woods makes it easy to feel that it is 1846 and that Thoreau is just across the woods a piece. You might not want to pay him a visit, but that is not the point. The point is that in such a setting you can tune him in and out at will with greater clarity because his signals, so to speak, are coming from a nearer location. Your pupils have dilated as the light gradually thins out and grows dim, so that when you can no longer make out the words, you look up and are surprised that early evening is upon you. It is time to get up and go home to dinner. How long had you been sitting there? An hour? Three hours? Since 1846?

Such extended periods of absorption are more difficult in towns and cities, where the hubbub of daily life constantly reminds you that time is passing, passing in fits and starts. You sit in your easy chair, reading a book. A police car goes by, its siren wobbling out extraterrestrial frequencies. You notice and wonder, "Going where?" You get back into the book. The phone rings. Who'd be calling you at two in the afternoon? "Are you busy?" No, just reading. Finally you go back to your book for a while. The kids across the hall come home from school. Bang bang on the door. *"Mami, apra la puerta!"* It must be 3:10 or so. And so on. Each break in concentration is a reminder that time is passing, what we might call "real" time. The flow of time in the book will not have real time in it. The farther we are from real time, the more likely it is that we will be able to become fully absorbed in the flow of time in the book.

Reading a book such as *Walden* in the woods is more complete not only because the setting is sympathetic, but also because it is conducive to timelessness. As Thoreau put it,

> The oldest Egyptian or Hindu philosopher raised a corner of the veil from the statue of the divinity; and still the trembling robe remains raised, and I gaze upon as fresh a glory as he did, since it was I in him that was then so bold, and it is he in me that now reviews the vision. No dust has settled on that robe; no time has elapsed since that divinity was revealed. That time which we really improve, or which is improvable, is neither past, present, nor future.
>
> My residence was more favorable, not only to thought, but to serious reading, than a university. . . . (352)

What is the urban correlative? How do we read an urban novel among urban "vibrations," but with a sense of timelessness? By reading very late at night or very early in the morning, when time "means" less. Going to college in New York City, I often stayed up all night reading, going out for coffee or a stroll just before dawn, when the streets were empty, cool, and quiet. It is a time of day that psychologically is outside of time: the old night is not yet over and the new day not yet begun. It was around this "no-time" that I seemed to read with the greatest absorption.

Do you read best at a certain time of day? How long has this been true? Within the past few years, have you tried reading at times you wouldn't normally consider? How about getting up earlier than usual and reading before you "start" the day? Or try carrying a book with you everywhere you go, and reading it at every slack moment.

You might also try matching up your reading material with where you read it (*The Old Man and the Sea* at the beach, for instance). You might also want to have the book go *against* the grain of where you read it; for example, read the Bible in a topless bar. Charles Lamb provides a less extreme example: "I should not care to be caught in the serious avenues of some cathedral alone, and reading *Candide*" (149). Does the location change the feel of the book? If so, how? Are you more comfortable reading with the grain or against it? Or neither?

Finally, to push matters further, you might want to explore other unusual reading situations: at a concert, when slightly ill, during a violent storm, when you're so depressed you don't feel like doing *anything*, under hypnosis, while drifting alone in a boat, while riding a Ferris wheel, or while standing on your head. One reader reported that, in fact, the only way he was able to visualize the upside-down ship in *The Poseidon Adventure* was by lying on his back on the floor while holding the book above him, "so that [he] was like the passengers were" (Nell 291). I wonder what it's like to read while floating in outer space.

10 Other Faces

Most people read without noticing the "look" of what they're reading. They don't notice the typeface or the page design. This is not to say that the look doesn't affect the reader. It does. The reader's response is unconscious, and therefore all the more subject to manipulation. "When we print a word in black ink on a rectangle of white paper, we are creating a composition in black and white," writes Marshall Lee in his *Bookmaking* (87). Whether brilliant, ordinary, or execrable, *any* composition has character: strong or weak, dynamic or inert, quiet or noisy, classy or tacky. We react to these qualities; the more knowledgeable we are, the more discriminating our reaction. In characterizing different typefaces, a child learning to read would not show the same discrimination as an expert such as Marshall Lee:

> Type faces—like people's faces—have distinctive features indicating aspects of character. Some features are quite pronounced, some are very subtle and subject to individual interpretation. Here are some text faces with capsule character analyses.
>
> > *Baskerville*—Classical and elegant
> > *Jason*—Round and warm
> > *Granjon*—Round, warm, and graceful
> > *Caledonia*—Clean, firm, businesslike
> > *Times Roman*—Stiff, cold, formal
> > *Electra*—Light, cool, efficient
> > *Fairfield*—Fussy
> > *Bodoni*—Dramatic
> > *Waverly*—Round and cool
>
> (78)

If you don't know anything about typefaces, such characterizations might sound a little *too* refined. Lee admits that such interpretations are always subjective. But the more one studies the typefaces listed above, the more accurate Lee's descriptions seem. But whether or not you agree with his interpretation, it can hardly be disputed that typefaces have character, and that the reader senses that character while reading.

Take, as an extreme example, the same word set in two quite different faces:

𝕭𝖊𝖗𝖑𝖎𝖓   Berlin

To readers of my generation, the first *Berlin* probably conjures up dark images of Nazi Germany; by comparison the second *Berlin* looks harmless.

Here's another example:

Vienna   Vienna

Which looks better to you; that is, more appropriate? Probably the script version, which calls up pleasant associations of nineteenth-century Austria, Strauss waltzes, elegant, aristocratic balls in sparkling palaces—the very associations we hope to invoke by sending out similarly engraved wedding invitations.

When I graduated from college, I received a diploma printed on high-quality paper and using a very distinguished, classical typeface. The words were in Latin. Accompanying it was an English translation, mimeographed on cheap paper that has long since turned sallow. The oil in the mimeograph ink has slowly "bled" into the sheet, blurring the words. These two pieces of paper serve as a paradigm of snobbism. They speak volumes, and we don't even have to know what the words are! If you understand the Latin, you join the elite; if you don't, you may count yourself as, well, common.

At one time or another, you have no doubt received from a friend a letter that was printed on a dot-matrix printer. You know the kind of words I mean: they're made of lots of little dots, they look sort of blurry, and they sometimes have a *g* or a *y* that looks funny. Doesn't a letter in this form feel impersonal, even robotic? Aren't you a little put off by it? No matter what the letter says, it won't seem as special as one written by hand, or even typewritten, because these last two, at least, will be the only first copy. The computer letter could be printed out again and again, with every copy looking exactly like every other copy: a clone.

The same goes for form letters. Such letters give you the feeling that they aren't really for you; they aren't for anyone in particular. Advertisers and others soliciting your business by direct mail know all this, of course, and they try to distract you by adding little "personal" touches. One thing they do is to have the letter's signature printed in a different color, usually blue. They don't really think that we will believe that Joe Blow actually sat down and signed 2.6 million copies of this letter; no, they're just counting on the softening effect of such a signature. Test mailings have confirmed the effectiveness of this method.

Another thing advertisers do is send you a computer-generated letter with your name imbedded at various points in the text:

> You'll be amazed, Mr. Ronald Padgett, at the effectiveness of this revolutionary new leaf blower. If, after a *free* 30-day trial in the privacy of your own home, you are not completely satisfied, Mr. Padgett, we will cheerfully refund your money. We're so sure, though,

that you, Mr. Padgett, will be overjoyed by this revolutionary new
leaf blower. . . .

And so on. Now, I would like to meet the rare bird who would believe
that such letters are individually typed. But no matter how physically ugly
and unconvincing such letters are, they do contain some of the most
powerful and effective words we know—our own names. The advertiser
is counting on that power to get us to read the pitch, despite the negative
effects of the computer-generated type.

The more we see dot-matrix type, the less offensive it seems. Not
because it *is* less offensive, but because it becomes customary. This is
true of any typeface. It is also true that we find it easier to read typefaces
we're accustomed to. Children who are just beginning to read on their
own find it difficult to read small type, partly because large letters are easier to recognize, partly because children are accustomed to large type.
Marshall Lee has noted (91) that American publishers print readers for
children ages 5–7 in type about 18 points high. (The "point" is a unit of
measure in typesetting; there are 72 points per inch.) The large type is a
signal for the children that this is, in fact, a children's book. To accommo-
date the large letters, there will be few words on each page, or the page
will be large, or both.

If the page is large, the book shouldn't have too many of them, lest
the book become unwieldy for little hands. I wish publishers would show
the same consideration to adult readers. Many's the time I have at-
tempted, while reading in bed, to rest a weighty tome on my belly, only to
find myself later in the throes of gastritis. Per cubic inch, books are surprisingly heavy.

Especially those with glossy pages, such as illustrated textbooks
and school yearbooks. One of the agonies of junior high school was having to lug home what seemed like a mountain of textbooks, switching
them from arm to arm to relieve the fatigue. For me, the glossy textbooks
added the visual torture of glare: coated paper is better for printing reproductions, but it reflects light something awful.

Marshall Lee lists nine factors that, content aside, determine a
page's readability:

1. typeface
2. size of type
3. length of line
4. leading (pronounced "ledding," the amount of space between
   lines)

5. page pattern
6. contrast of type and paper
7. texture of paper
8. typographical relationships (chapter heads, page numbers, etc.)
9. suitability of content.

Perhaps the most pernicious of these is excessive line length. In Figure 26 I've quoted Lee (92) on this subject, but I've intentionally made the lines too long. Lee estimates that, at the normal book-reading distance of about 16 inches, the maximum comfortable line length is about 5 inches. The further beyond that you go, the less readable the material is.

Finally, the well-designed page has a characteristic that only an articulate artist or typographical expert such as Lee would notice:

> In a well-designed page, the white areas are effective elements interacting with the black—the page is alive. In poor typography, the type seems printed on *top* of a white background—the page is dead. (88)

This brings up the question of whether what we read is black on white or white around black. Obviously we can't have one without the other; but which of the two we focus on determines to some degree how we read. Some speed-readers suggest that reading the white is more fluid.

By going into some detail here about typefaces and book design, I am not suggesting that we all need to become experts on the subject. I do believe, though, that we will become better readers if we're more aware of the circumstances—sometimes the constraints—under which we read. Otherwise, in having trouble reading a poorly designed book, we may blame ourselves or the author for shortcomings that instead are the publisher's.

Children also blame themselves when they have trouble reading. A little voice in them says, "I can't do this, it's too hard for me." They are not in a position to know that the fault may lie elsewhere; that the content has no sparkle, no wit, no life; that stylistically it is stale, characterless, enervated; or that its typeface and design are uninviting. Nor can they know that other forces are causing their eyes to skitter off the page.

Many children—especially those who come to school from emotionally unstable homes in socially and economically ravaged neighborhoods, who come to school metabolically askew with poor nutrition, who come to school vibrating from the relentless hammering of urban life—have trouble just keeping their eyes on any one thing for an extended period of time. I'm not talking about the short attention span that is common to infants. I'm talking about children who cannot keep their

Tests have shown many disadvantages in long lines: (a) the eye must blink at intervals during reading. After each blink, an optical adjustment and refocus takes place. The longer the line, the more frequently blinks occur within, rather than at the end of lines; (b) there is the time and visual effort lost in traveling back to the beginning of the next line; (c) when the measure is too wide, there is momentary difficulty in determining which *is* the next line (sometimes the wrong one is selected). Each interruption—the blink, the trip back, and the search for the right line—causes loss of reading efficiency, or poor readability. (Lee, p. 92)

Figure 26. Long lines example.

eyes on anything that doesn't constantly move around and entertain them, that doesn't feed them "eye-candy"—children who have grown up with television as part of their nervous systems.

Put the emphasis on *systems* and you'll see what I mean: the systems are nervous. They are nervous because they have been subjected to a constant bombardment of excitations and irritations from the cathode ray tube that projects images that jump and switch and cut away every few seconds. Try this experiment. Go turn on your television set. Turn the sound off. Look at the second hand on your watch. Watch the screen for one minute. Count the number of times the view is switched. If the show is an "adult" show, such as *Meet the Press*, it won't jump around so much. If it's a comedy series, it'll jump around a lot. If it's a cartoon, it'll jump around a lot. If it's a commercial, it'll jump around like crazy. What would you guess is the average amount of time that a particular camera shot is left on the screen? I'm writing this with a word processor hooked up to my television, so I can switch back and forth between these words and the various stations. I just switched over to Channel 4 (NBC). Commercials. The visual phrasing was staccato, with each shot lasting only two or three seconds. What, I wondered, would it be like if I began to see everything this way? I looked over at the plants on the windowsill, jumped to John Kenneth Galbraith's *Money* on the shelf, jumped to the glass of paintbrushes behind it, jumped to the wall, jumped to the painting on the wall, jumped to the record cabinet, jumped to the chair, ugh! It was awful, and the idea of doing it nonstop for a couple of hours was unbearable. Try it for a few minutes. You'll find that you glaze over quickly, unable to concentrate on any of the things your eyes land on. On most television shows, of course, the concentrating is done for you. The result is that all too often one becomes a passive lump with a hazed brain and an agitated nervous system. So what's surprising about the fact that many schoolchildren cannot chin themselves, remember what they're told, or concentrate?

I'm sure there are statistics on the relative amount of jumping around on various types of television shows, and there may even be statistics comparing today's jumpiness to that of, say, 25 years ago. My gut sense of it is that today's programming is much jumpier. I remember going to see "avant-garde," "underground" American films in 1960 that had very quick cutting, so quick that they seemed almost abstract. In comparison, commercial cinema seemed to lumber along. What was considered avant-garde cutting in 1960 is now the order of the day. This high-speed zigzag imagery is pouring into children's nervous systems for hours every day. According to the Department of Education's *What Works: Research About Teaching and Learning*, "At home, half of all fifth graders spend . . . an average of 130 minutes a day watching television" (11). The same fifth graders spend "only four minutes a day reading." I don't know how such statistics are arrived at, I don't think television is inherently evil, and I'm not against quick cutting as an artistic technique. I'm just saying it's dishonest to allow our children to be accelerated into a visual and visceral blur, and then to blame the schools for their reading problems. Nor should we allow our children to blame themselves.

For decades, teachers and reading specialists have been warning us about the dangers of television, and all too often, I suspect, their cavils have been dismissed as those of the old biddy and the wet blanket. Hey, a little TV can't hurt anybody, can it? No, a little can't. But television is like peanuts: you can't eat just one. Before you know it, you're down to the bottom of the jar and you don't feel so good. Finally, you turn off the set and stagger off to bed. You've watched a lot, but you've seen little, and you'll remember less. You are as far away from reading as possible.

How far away from reading are you when you do read? Or rather, how far away is what you read? Consider the following situation:

> When a driver approaches an intersection, an automobile from the right appears to be moving at a much faster pace than actually is the case. This is an optical illusion produced by the action of the two cars approaching the intersection at about the same time. Often, when the auto from the right travels toward the center of the street, it seems to speed up, but actually it may be slowing down. (Hovious 176)

This situation is diagrammed in Figure 27. Imagine yourself as the driver of car D. The car marked R appears to be speeding up, in the spot marked by the dotted line.

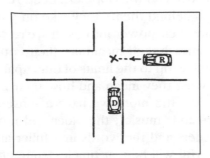

Figure 27. Cars at intersection.

Is there a similar phenomenon in the act of reading? That is, is the reader like the driver in car D, and the approaching words like car R?

The reader's peripheral vision includes the words approaching from the right (or at least seem to be approaching. Of course the words aren't moving; the eyes are. But the effect is the same as if the eyes were stationary and the words moving from right to left.) As the eyes move from left to right across a line of type, the words to the far right seem to pick up speed as they approach the point of fixation, where, for an instant, they stand still, before zooming away to the left. This visual illusion of the words speeding up as they approach and slowing down as they recede is comparable to the Doppler Effect.

The Doppler Effect is one of those phenomena that are so familiar that we rarely realize they happen. Imagine you are standing alongside a flat stretch of highway in the middle of the desert. It is dead quiet. Then, far down the road, you see a speck, a dot of color approaching: it's a car. As the car approaches, the dull growl of its engine rises to a shrill whine until—whrooom!—the car blows past you, and the pitch of its engine falls and fades to silence. It's as if the the sound had disappeared, the way lines of perspective disappear into the vanishing point.* So, in the distance, the car seems small and slow, with an engine sound that is low in volume and pitch. Up close, the car is big and fast, with a loud, high-pitched engine. One difference between looking at a car approach and reading a line of words is that we can keep our eyes focused on the car throughout the entire process, whereas we have to leap from word-group to word-group, refocusing and pausing each time. That's why the words don't seem to move when we're fixated on them. It's as if they've entered—for that instant—a timeless zone, the zone our eyes are fixated on, the zone our minds are (presumably) in.

I want to suggest that, in reading, there is a psychological equivalent to the laws of perspective and the Doppler Effect. As the words approach the eye (and the mind behind them), they take on a momentousness that allows them to radiate their power into us. If we're reading with our full faculties, the words unleash their meanings, their connotations, their sensuality, their whole being, up to the limits of our capabilities. The more we know about words, what they mean and how their meanings shift when they're set side by side; the more we have a sense of the "feel" of the words, their textures and "music"; the older and more experienced we are, more able to understand the words in a fuller and richer context— then, the more powerful will be that timeless, immobile moment of fixation, when the purest transportation occurs.

----

*If Renaissance Italians discovered perspective in art, who discovered "perspective" in sound?

Appendix: Skywriting

I t was a bright warm spring afternoon around 1952, and there must have been advance word, because quite a few people on our tree-lined street were outdoors, scanning the skies. Around two o'clock, the first puff appeared in the sky, the beginning of a graceful, looping rope of "smoke" that veered this way and that, writing an immense white message across the pure blue sky. It might have said something as mundane as EAT AT JOE'S, but that didn't matter, for, as the pianist Glenn Gould said about the first radio broadcast, what mattered was not *what* was said, but rather that a miracle was happening. In this case, the miracle was that large words appeared in the heavens. Then the sky rained down hundreds and hundreds of balloons that fell like big drifting raindrops and came to rest all across town. Inside the balloon I caught was a certificate for a free carton of soda pop. It was Tulsa's version of manna from heaven.

I never fail to see words written in the sky without being moved, perhaps because of this early experience, perhaps because of something deeper, and invariably I pause to watch the entire message until it is erased by the wind. Its delicacy, rarity, and brief existence make it all the more precious, no matter what it says. In fact, I confess that although I read the messages, I forget them even before they fade from the sky.

If you ask older New Yorkers if they remember any skywriting from the late 1930s—about 60 years ago—many will promptly mention Pepsi Cola and the I. J. Fox Fur Company. I have similar memories instilled in me by another delightful advertising technique, memories of Burma Shave, a product I would use, out of sheer gratitude, were it still on the market. Those clever Burma Shave jingles, with each line on a separate sign placed at intervals alongside the road—intervals just right for leisurely reading at 50 miles per hour—may have been what predisposed me to "experimental" writing.[1] But no terrestrial writing gives me the timeless, hypnotic feeling that skywriting does.

During World War I, airplanes laid down smoke screens along the trenches to disguise infantry assaults, and from this practice came the idea of skywriting. The smoke was created by pouring oil into the engine manifold. The hot engine burned the oil and created a dark smoke. The first skywriter was Major John S. Savage of the Royal Air Force, who used skywriting to send war messages over great distances when other means were not possible.[2] The first commercial use of skywriting was by Captain Cyril Turner, also an RAF pilot, who skywrote over Epsom Downs during the English Derby in May of 1922.[3] Captain Allen J. Cameron, an American pilot, saw the demonstration that day and brought the technique to America. His first message, written over New York City in October of 1922, was HELLO USA. The popularity of skywriting as an advertising medium increased until World War II, when pilots, planes, and other resources were diverted into the war effort. Skywriting resumed after the war, but was dealt an even heavier blow in the late 1940s by the advent of television advertising. It was as though the big blue sky had been replaced by the little blue tube. Throughout the 1950s, skywriting retreated to large metropolitan areas, where a lot of people tended to be outdoors in nice weather; to sporting events, such as the Rose Bowl, where a large, captive audience could be reached; and to the company that had a history of skywriting advertising, Pepsi-Cola. Not counting a lone individual here and there, by the 1980s there were only four skywriting agencies in the U.S.: Skytypers West (in California), Skytypers East (in New York), Rosie O'Grady's Flying Circus (in Florida), and the Pepsi-Cola Company, and even Pepsi had a long skywriting hiatus (1953–1975).

When Pepsi resumed its skywriting, it used only one plane, a 1929 Travel Air D4D open-cockpit biplane. Since 1981, it has been piloted by the only female skywriter, Suzanne Asbury-Oliver. She is also the only Pepsi skywriter, and, discounting the occasional outside job, PEPSI is all she writes.

Pepsi got the Travel Air in 1973 from Anthony "Andy" Stinis, who thought the company wanted it as a piece of corporate memorabilia. Stinis, one of the original Pepsi skywriters, had used that very plane writing more than 7,000 Pepsi messages from 1938 until 1953, when Pepsi began its hiatus. He had done his first skywriting in the early 1930s. Apparently he was something of a daredevil. His son Greg speculates that skywriting was the natural result of his father's love of flying—he was there when Charles Lindbergh took off on his historic transatlantic flight—and racing motorcycles. Andy had some interesting skywriting experiences, such as writing a whiskey ad in the night sky (presumably with a bright moon illuminating the letters from behind): true moonshine. After his stint with Pepsi, Andy continued with his own skywriting company, Stinis Air Services, which changed its name to Skytypers in 1979. He holds the patent to the skywriting method he invented in 1949, called *skytyping*.

Sky*writing* is still done pretty much the way it was in World War I. Today, however, the skywriting fluid is an "environmentally approved" (as every skywriter will hasten to inform you) oil-base solution, a petroleum byproduct that doesn't dissipate as quickly as straight water vapor. The fluid is released into the plane's manifold exhaust collector ring, where the engine heat vaporizes it into a white "smoke" that is then emitted from a pipe and expands into big white lines.

Skywriting is usually done in block letters by a single plane. Apparently it's not that easy to learn. A few years ago, Greg Stinis, the operator of Skytypers West, trained seasoned pilots for a big skywriting job across the western U.S.: 65 cities in 10 days. Each pilot had 10–15 years' experience with the planes—SNJ-2s—and were given carefully planned instruction. It took them two to three weeks to learn to skywrite, and even then their "handwriting" was childlike. Continuous script is much more difficult. According to Greg Stinis, skywriting is somewhat instinctive. You have to develop a feel for it, in your body, as you're forming the letters.[4] "Everything you're doing is behind you. You have to develop a kind of sixth sense on how to do it," he says. However, there are some tricks of the trade. For instance, before you start the message, you pick some highly visible landmarks, which serve as a baseline for the message, like lines on ruled paper. Before the flight, most skywriters diagram the message on a piece of paper or cardboard, with arrows and symbols indicating the direction of the turns and pauses, and keep the diagram in the cockpit. The diagram reads upside down and backwards, because that's the way the message looks from the point of view of the pilot. Most pilots count silently as they form the various parts of the letters, the way ballet dancers count measures to keep track of where they are in a piece of choreography. If the pilot gets worried about the alignment of the letters, he can roll out a little and take a peek. Also, if the conditions are just right, he can use the sun to see shadows on the ground, the shadows of the words he's writing.

The shadows are likely to be quite visible, because the letters are from three-quarters to one mile tall, probably the largest letters on earth (so to speak). Placed at an altitude of 10,000 feet, they can be read from 20–50 miles away.

Wind, haze, and overcast skies are the skywriter's *bêtes noires*. Because much of the skywriter's cost is simply getting up in the air and getting down, he or she frequently checks the weather bureau for conditions at 10,000 feet, especially wind velocity. Wind is particularly bad for skywriting. As Mort Arken, head of Skytypers East, explained, "In skywriting, it takes a single plane at least ten minutes to form the letters in SOLARCAINE. By the time the pilot has written the E, the S, O, and L have faded and the rest of the letters are disappearing."[5]

This is why Andy Stinis's invention of sky*typing* was a great advance in efficiency: it is faster, and therefore can handle longer messages. SOLARCAINE can be skytyped in 45 seconds—about 4 seconds per letter. Therefore, skytyping can be done on windier days. Skytyping is the exclusive service of Skytypers East, which Stinis handed on to Mort Arken, and of Skytypers West. In skytyping, five planes (SNJ–2s, military planes built in the early 1940s) fly side by side, around 250 feet apart. The lead plane, in the center, contains a computer that sends radio signals to smoke-producing devices on all five planes, telling them when to emit puffs of smoke. Thus, in forming the letter O, each of the five planes will first emit a puff simultaneously. It will look like this:

```
                                  -
                                  -
                                  -
                                  -
                                  -
```

Then only the two end planes will emit some puffs, forming the top and bottom of the letter:

```
                              - - - -
                                  -
                                  -
                                  -
                              - - - -
```

Finally, all five will again emit puffs, to form the final side:

```
                              - - - - -
                                -     -
                                -     -
                                -     -
                              - - - - -
```

The result is boxy, but practical. The principle is the same as that of the dot-matrix printing of computers and electronic typewriters. It isn't elegant, but it's ingenious and fast.

Given to nostalgia, I prefer the slow elegance of skywriting, preferably in script. I get little pleasure from watching people type, but for some reason I enjoy watching people write: the flow of words onto paper has always fascinated me (the words of others, that is). And with drawing, the experience is even more intense: when I watch my artist friends draw, I get a tingly, dreamy, happy feeling. So what about skydrawing? And couldn't short poems be written across the sky by jets?[6]

Notes

Chapter 2

1. As Don Holdaway points out, though, the focus has been on how to teach reading, with little attention paid to how reading is *learned* (see *The Foundations of Literacy* 15).

2. See, for example, *How to Teach Your Baby to Read* by Glen J. Doman.

3. Don Holdaway's *Foundations of Literacy* has some wonderful passages on the lack of empowerment of students, such as: "The child who is humiliated by his failure to carry out an analytic process which even his own teacher is incapable of performing unerringly, such as syllabification, ought to have the right to massive legal compensation" (p. 103).

4. See Ellen Lupton's delightful and imaginative essay, "An Abbreviated History of Punctuation," in *Educating the Imagination,* edited by Christopher Edgar and Ron Padgett.

5. See *The Complete Guide to Punctuation* by Margaret Enright Wye, p. 34.

6. Ann Lauterbach's poem "Betty Observed" (in her *Before Recollection*) makes a similar point:

When I was young, I used to
Check pages for talk; dialogue was the key
To readability. That was before I had a taste
For abstraction. "I love you Betty" was a good sign

Chapter 5

1. Our system of reading horizontally came from the ancient Greeks. Their method was a bit different, though. Greek was originally written in a pattern called *boustrophedon* ("as the ox turns"), with the eye following the same path as an ox plowing a field:

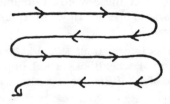

In other words, Greek was read from left to right to left to right and so on. For more information, see *Dyslexia and Your Child* by Rudolph F. Wagner. Later the Greek pattern changed to the left-to-right pattern we use.

2. Don Holdaway has an interesting discussion of this idea in his *Foundations of Literacy*, pp. 96–98.

3. Frank Kermode discusses this interview in his *Genesis of Secrecy*, p. 13.

4. See Frank Smith's *Reading without Nonsense* for an interesting discussion of the role of anticipation in reading.

Chapter 6

1. See Kenneth Koch's translation of part of it, in Roussel's *How I Wrote Certain of My Books* (Boston: Exact Change, 1995), an expanded version of the same title published by SUN in New York in 1977.

2. See *But I Digress*, an interesting study of the use of parentheses in English verse, by John Lennard.

3. An even smoother—and a devilishly clever—example is one (ca. 1600) that was written expressly to be read both vertically and cross-column:

I holde as faythe	What Englands Church allowes
What Romes church saith	My conscience disallowes
Where the King is head	The church can have no shame
The flock's mislead	That hath the Pope Supreame
Where the Altar's drest	Ther's service scarce divine
The People's Blest	With Table, Bread and Wine
He's but as Asse	Who that Com[m]union flyes
Who shun's the mass	Is Catholique and wise
Wherefore I pray	The England flourish best
That Rome may sway	Shall ne'er be my request

(Folger Shakespeare Library, Washington, D.C. [MS V.a. 198, fol. 14^r], quoted in Lennard 266–67)

Lennard also mentions a poem in Latin that "reads forwards and backwards, each direction providing a different meaning" (267).

4. In an interview on "The Printed Word and Beyond," part of WNET's "Innovation" series broadcast January 7, 1988.

5. Interview in *Paris Review* No. 35, 1965, p. 24. It is interesting to note that collage or cut-up writing often seems to have more than one voice in it, and that Eliot's poem is, in fact, the product not only of collaged material but also of strong editorial excisions by another poet, Ezra Pound.

6. The night after I wrote these words, I dreamed I was reading a letter, but when, in the dream, I said to myself, "Hey, I'm reading in a dream," the words grew blurry and disappeared.

7. My source for this information, *Ripley's Believe It or Not 50th Anniversary Edition* (New York: Pocket Books, 1968, unpaginated, no author credited) does not give the date of *Nihil: Rien* or its author's first name.

Chapter 8

1. At a recent lecture–demonstration by the head of a CD-ROM company, a member of the audience asked a disarming question: "Does anybody actually

read CD-ROMs?" The implication was that CD-ROMs sometimes have wonderful combinations of graphics, sound, and text, but that their text comes in a far distant third. Who would really want to read, for example, *Moby-Dick* from a computer monitor? It's not just that prolonged staring at a cathode ray tube can make you feel that masonry nails have been driven into your eyes; it's also that the monitor is a glass wall between reader and text, a text that remains distant and cool. Reading a book is more intimate partly because it's more sensuous. You can hold and caress a book, and when it's new, you can even sniff its heady combination of printer's ink, binding glue, and fresh paper, and when the book grows old, its ineffable essence of library. Books are like food. Will we ever "devour" a CD-ROM? As for reading in bed. . . .

2. From Guillaume Apollinaire's poem "Zone" in Koch and Farrell, p. 123 (my translation).

3. An awareness of sign language and modern dance can expand our definition of reading. Peter Wisher, a coach and professor of physical education at Gallaudet University (the school for the deaf), created a new form of dance for his students. When viewed by a hearing audience, Wisher's choreography simply seems to include large gestures, but to deaf audiences who know American Sign Language, the dance is also operatic, because the dancers are actually signing the lyrics with their entire bodies. Years before I learned of Wisher's work, I wrote, in a poem: "I am saying / that grammar is the direct result of how humans feel in the world; / or rather, / that grammar follows from what we experience viscerally and punctuation keeps it that way; / that, for instance, people walking down the street are forming various sentences with their bodies. . . ." ("Yak and Yak," *New & Selected Poems* 15). See also my article "Phrases in Grammar and Dance," in which I discuss the relationship between the phrase in dance and the phrase in language. Many choreographers of modern dance are aware of such relationships between dance and language, and that in some way, perhaps unconsciously, their dances can be "read." Such relationships have been the subject of study for many years by bee experts such as Karl von Frisch, author of *The Dancing Bees*.

4. Unpublished poem, written in a poetry class conducted by Judith Steinbergh.

Chapter 9

1. Some people, such as Charles Lamb, find *any* outdoor reading impossible: "I am not much a friend to out-of-door reading. I cannot settle my spirits to it." From "Detached Thoughts on Books and Reading" (149).

Appendix

1. For more information on Burma Shave signs, see *The Verse by the Side of the Road* by Frank Rowsome.

2. I mean skywriting in the modern sense of the word. Otherwise, it could be argued that Native American smoke signals constituted the first skywriting.

3. *Webster's Ninth New Collegiate Dictionary* gives 1922 as the year of the first known use of the word *skywriting*, but one wonders what it was called before then.

4. To get some idea of what is meant here, try these experiments. At the beach, find a large area where the sand is smooth. First, use a stick to write a very large (perhaps 30 feet high) message in the sand, with your eyes closed. Second, write a large message with your eyes open, but trailing the stick behind you, and forming the letters upside-down and backwards.

5. Quoted in *The New Yorker*'s "Talk of the Town" column, July 17, 1978, issue. The May 28, 1987, *Wall Street Journal* also has an interesting article about skywriting, entitled "Last Few Skywriters Strut the Stuff Doing Ads on the Fly."

6. I like the idea of ending a book in a footnote. It turns out that someone *has* written poems across the sky. A few years ago, David Antin created such poems, a three-line one over Santa Monica and a four-line one over La Jolla, California. Limited to around 20 letters per line because of wind dispersal, Antin played on the idea of erasure by using several short phrases in each line, phrases whose meanings toyed with the reader's expectations. In radio contact on the ground, Antin told the pilots of Skytypers West to wait until each line disappeared before writing the next. For a fuller description and a photograph, see his article "Fine Furs" in *Critical Inquiry*.

Bibliography

This bibliography includes works cited and works that were in a more general way useful in the writing of this book.

Agnes, Yves, and Jean-Michel Croissandeau. *Lire le journal*. St-Julien-du-Sault, France: F. P. Lobies, 1979.

Antin, David. "Fine Furs." *Critical Inquiry* 19.1 (Autumn 1992): 155–63.

Aristotle. "On the Art of Poetry." *Classical Literary Criticism*. Ed. and trans. T. S. Dorsch. New York: Penguin, 1984.

Barthes, Roland. *The Pleasure of the Text*. Trans. Richard Miller. New York: Farrar, Straus & Giroux, 1975.

Berger, Allen. *Speed Reading: An Annotated Bibliography*. Newark: International Reading Association, 1970.

Berrigan, Ted. *Clear the Range*. New York: Adventures in Poetry/Coach House, 1977.

———. *The Sonnets*. 3rd ed. New York: United Artists, 1982.

Berthoff, Ann E. *Forming Thinking Writing: The Composing Imagination*. Montclair: Boynton/Cook, 1982.

Bettelheim, Bruno, and Karen Zelan. *On Learning to Read: The Child's Fascination with Meaning*. New York: Knopf, 1982.

Billington, Lillian E. *Using Words*. New York: Silver Burdett, 1945.

Blanchot, Maurice. *The Gaze of Orpheus*. Trans. Lydia Davis. Barrytown: Station Hill, 1981.

Bloomfield, Leonard. *Language*. New York: Henry Holt, 1933.

Bornstein, Diane. *A History of the English Language*. Booklet accompanying a boxed set of three lp phonograph records of the same name. New York: Caedmon Records, 1973.

Bruner, Jerome. *The Process of Education*. Cambridge: Harvard University Press, 1965.

Burroughs, William. Interview. *Paris Review* no. 35, 1965.

Burroughs, William, and Brion Gysin. *The Third Mind*. New York: Viking, 1978.

Caws, Mary Ann. *The Art of Interference*. Princeton: Princeton University Press, 1989.

———. *The Eye in the Text: Essays on Perception, Mannerist to Modern*. Princeton: Princeton University Press, 1981.

Césaire, Aimé. *The Collected Poetry*. Trans. Clayton Eshleman and Annette Smith. Berkeley & Los Angeles: University of California Press, 1983.

Chall, Jeanne S. *Learning to Read: The Great Debate*. 2nd ed. New York: Mc-Graw-Hill, 1983.

——. *Stages of Reading Development*. New York: McGraw-Hill, 1983.

Chase, Stuart. *The Tyranny of Words*. New York: Harcourt Brace Jovanovich, 1959.

Chomsky, Noam. *Syntactic Structures*. The Hague: Mouton, 1957.

Cole, K. C. *Vision: In the Eye of the Beholder*. San Francisco: Exploratorium, 1978.

Commission on Reading. *Becoming a Nation of Readers*. Washington: National Institute of Education, 1985.

Covino, William A. *The Art of Wondering*. Portsmouth: Boynton/Cook, 1988.

Crowder, Robert G. *The Psychology of Reading*. New York: Oxford University Press, 1982.

Davis, Bonnie M. *A Guide to Information Sources for Reading*. Newark: International Reading Association, 1972.

De Bono, Edward. *Lateral Thinking*. London: Ward Lock Educational, 1970.

——. *The Use of Lateral Thinking*. London: Jonathan Cape, 1967.

Denby, Edwin. *Complete Poems*. New York: Random House, 1986.

Disch, Thomas M. *Amnesia*. Computer disk. San Mateo: Electronic Arts, 1986.

Doman, Glenn J. *How to Teach Your Baby to Read*. Garden City: Doubleday, 1975.

Dorsch, T. S., ed. and trans. *Classical Literary Criticism*. New York: Penguin, 1986.

Durkin, Dolores. *Children Who Read Early*. New York: Teachers College Press, 1966.

——. *Teaching Them to Read*. Boston: Allyn & Bacon, 1970.

Edgar, Christopher, and Ron Padgett. *Educating the Imagination*. 2 vols. New York: Teachers & Writers Collaborative, 1994. [Ellen Lupton's essay on the history of punctuation is in volume 1.]

Engel, Susan. *The Stories Children Tell*. New York: W. H. Freeman, 1995.

Freud, Sigmund. *The Basic Writings of Sigmund Freud*. Ed. and trans. A. A. Brill. New York: Modern Library, 1938.

Frisch, Karl von. *The Dancing Bees*. New York: Harcourt, Brace, 1953.

Goodman, Ken. *On Reading*. Portsmouth: Heinemann, 1996.

——. *What's Whole in Whole Language?* Portsmouth: Heinemann, 1986.

Goodman, Yetta, and Carolyn Burke. *Reading Miscue Inventory: Procedure for Diagnosis and Evaluation*. New York: Macmillan, 1972.

Gray, William S., and Marion Monroe. *Think-and-Do Book*. Chicago: Scott, Foresman, 1946.

Green, Henry. Interview. *Writers at Work: The Paris Review Interviews, Fifth Series*. Ed. George Plimpton. New York: Viking, 1981.

Grigson, Geoffrey. *The Faber Book of Nonsense*. London: Faber & Faber, 1979.

Hansen, Jane, Thomas Newkirk, and Donald Graves, eds. *Breaking Ground: Teachers Relate Reading and Writing in the Elementary School*. Portsmouth: Heinemann, 1985.

Hazlitt, William. "On the Pleasure of Hating" and "On Reading Old Books." *Selected Essays*. New York: Random House, 1930.

Hogben, Lancelot. *The Mother Tongue*. New York: Norton, 1965.

Holdaway, Don. *The Foundations of Literacy*. Sydney: Ashton Scholastic, 1979.

Hoover, Paul. *Idea*. Great Barrington: The Figures, 1987.

Hovious, Carol. *Following Printed Trails*. New York: Heath, 1936.

Huizinga, Jan. *Homo Ludens: A Study of the Play-Element in Culture*. Boston: Beacon Press, 1955.

Iser, Wolfgang. *The Act of Reading: A Theory of Aesthetic Response*. Baltimore: Johns Hopkins University Press, 1978.

———. *The Implied Reader*. Baltimore: Johns Hopkins University Press, 1974.

Jones, Richard M. *Fantasy and Feeling in Education*. New York: New York University Press, 1968.

Kaye, Peggy. *Games for Reading*. New York: Pantheon, 1984.

Keene, Carolyn, and Franklin W. Dixon. *The Secret of the Knight's Sword*. New York: Simon & Schuster, 1984.

Kermode, Frank. *The Genesis of Secrecy: On the Interpretation of Narrative*. Cambridge: Harvard University Press, 1979.

Koch, Kenneth, and Kate Farrell. *Sleeping on the Wing*. New York: Random House, 1981.

LaBerge, Stephen. *Lucid Dreaming*. Los Angeles: Tarcher, 1985.

Lakoff, George, and Mark Johnson. *Metaphors We Live By*. Chicago: University of Chicago, 1980.

Lamb, Charles. *The Complete Works and Letters of Charles Lamb*. New York: Modern Library, 1963.

Lauterbach, Ann. *Before Recollection*. Princeton: Princeton University Press, 1987.

Lee, Dorris, and R. V. Allen. *Learning to Read through Experience*. Englewood: Prentice-Hall, 1943, 1963.

Lee, Marshall. *Bookmaking*. 2nd ed. New York: Bowker, 1979.

Leites, Edmund. *The Puritan Conscience and Modern Sexuality*. New Haven: Yale University Press, 1986.

Lem, Stanislaw. *Chain of Chance*. Trans. Louis Iribane. New York: Harcourt Brace Jovanovich, 1978.

Lennard, Jim. *But I Digress*: *The Exploitation of Parentheses in English Printed Verse*. Oxford: Oxford University Press, 1991.

Loewinsohn, Ron. *Meat Air*. New York: Harcourt Brace Jovanovich, 1970.

Lupton, Ellen, ed. *Period Styles: A History of Punctuation*. Exhibition catalog. New York: Cooper Union, 1988. [Lupton's title essay reprinted in *Educating the Imagination,* vol. 1, ed. Christopher Edgar and Ron Padgett. New York: Teachers & Writers Collaborative, 1994.]

Mallarmé, Stéphane. *Un coup de dés n'abolira le hasard*. Trans. Daisy Aldan. New York: Tiber Press, 1956.

Meyer, Bonnie J. F., Carole J. Young, and Brendan J. Bartlett. *Memory Improved: Reading and Memory Enhancement across the Life Span through Strategic Text Strutures*. Hillsdale: Lawrence Erlbaum Associates, 1989.

Montaigne, Michel de. *Essays*. Trans. J. M. Cohen. New York: Penguin, 1981.

National Center for Education Statistics. *Digest of Education Statistics*. Washington: U. S. Government Printing Office, 1994.

National Commission on Excellence in Education. *A Nation at Risk*. Washington: U.S. Government Printing Office, 1983.

Nell, Victor. *Lost in a Book: The Psychology of Reading for Pleasure*. New Haven: Yale University Press, 1988.

Odier, Daniel. *The Job: Interviews with William Burroughs*. London: Cape, 1970.

Oulipo: Atlas de littérature potentielle. Paris: Gallimard, 1981. [An edited and expanded version of *Oulipo: La littérature potentielle*. Paris: Gallimard, 1973.]

Padgett, Ron. *Great Balls of Fire*. New York: Holt, Rinehart & Winston, 1969.

——. *New & Selected Poems*. Boston: David R. Godine, 1995.

——. "Phrases in Grammar and Dance." *Teachers & Writers* 18.2 Sept.–Oct. 1986.

——. "Problems with Words." *Blood Work*. Flint: Bamberger Books, 1993.

——. *Tulsa Kid*. Calais: Z Press, 1979.

——, ed. *The Teachers & Writers Handbook of Poetic Forms*. New York: Teachers & Writers Collaborative, 1987.

Pessoa, Fernando. *The Book of Disquiet*. Trans. Iain Watson. London: Quartet, 1991.

Picard, Michel. *La lecture comme jeu*. Paris: Editions de Minuit, 1986.

Plimpton, George, ed. *Writers at Work: The Paris Review Interviews, Fifth Series*. Interview with Henry Green by Terry Southern. New York: Viking, 1981.

——. *Writers at Work: The Paris Review Interviews, Third Series*. Interview with William Burroughs. New York: Penguin, 1977.

Queneau, Raymond. *Cent mille milliards de poèmes*. Paris: Gallimard, 1961.

Richards, I. A. *How to Read a Page*. New York: Norton, 1942.

————. *Practical Criticism*. San Diego: Harcourt Brace Jovanovich, n.d. (First published in 1929).

Rimbaud, Jean-Arthur. *A Season in Hell*. Trans. Delmore Schwartz. Norfolk: New Directions, 1939.

Ripley's Believe It or Not! 50th Anniversary Edition. New York: Pocket Books, 1968.

Robbe-Grillet, Alain. *The Voyeur*. Trans. Richard Howard. New York: Grove, 1958.

Rodari, Gianni. *The Grammar of Fantasy*. Trans. Jack Zipes. New York: Teachers & Writers Collaborative, 1996.

Rosenblatt, Louise. *The Reader, the Text, the Poem*. Carbondale: Southern Illinois University Press, 1978.

Roussel, Raymond. *How I Wrote Certain of My Books*. Trans. Trevor Winkfield. New York: SUN, 1977. [An expanded version was issued by Exact Change in 1995.]

Rowsome, Frank. *The Verse by the Side of the Road*. Brattleboro: Stephen Greene Press, 1965.

Saporta, Marc. *Composition No. 1*. Trans. Richard Howard. New York: Simon & Schuster, 1963.

Saroyan, Aram. [untitled]. New York: Kulchur, n.d.

Sartre, Jean-Paul. *The Words*. Trans. Bernard Frechtman. New York: George Braziller, 1964.

The Seeds and Other Stories. "A Night in 'Potato' Village" by Tai Mujen. Beijing: Foreign Language Press, 1972.

Shaughnessy, Mina P. *Errors and Expectations*. New York: Oxford University Press, 1977.

Smith, Frank. *Reading without Nonsense*. 2nd ed. New York: Teachers College Press, 1985.

————. *Understanding Reading*. Hillsdale: Lawrence Erlbaum Associates, 1986.

————, ed. *Psycholinguistics and Reading*. New York: Holt, Rinehart & Winston, 1973.

Smith, Nila Banton. *American Reading Instruction*. Newark: International Reading Association, 1986.

Smith, Thomas M. et al. *The Condition of Education*. Washington: U.S. Government Printing Office, 1994.

Spark, Muriel. *A Far Cry from Kensington*. Boston: Houghton Mifflin, 1988.

Spencer, Herbert, ed. *The Liberated Page*. San Francisco: Bedford Press, 1987.

Stein, Gertrude. *Selected Writings*. New York: Modern Library, 1962.

Taylor, Stanford Earl, Helen Frackenpohl, and James L. Pettee. *Grade Level Norms for the Components of the Fundamental Reading Skill*. Bulletin no. 3. Huntington: Educational Development Laboratories, 1960.

Thoreau, Henry David. *The Portable Thoreau*. Ed. by Carl Bode. New York: Penguin, 1981.

Touring Club Italiano. *Sicilia*. Milan: Touring Club Italiano, 1968.

Trelease, Jim. *The Read-Aloud Handbook*. New York: Penguin, 1982.

Tucker, Alan. *Reading Games*. Wymondham, England: Brewhouse, 1973.

Tzara, Tristan. *Lampisteries, precedés des Sept Manifestes Dada*. Paris: Jean-Jacques Pauvert, 1963. Trans. Barbara Wright as *Seven Dada Manifestos and Lampisteries*. London: Calder Publications, 1992.

United States National Commission on Excellence in Education. *A Nation at Risk*. Washington: U.S. Government Printing Office, 1983.

Vincent, Stephen, and Jayne Cortez, eds. *The Poetry Reading*. San Francisco: Momo's Press, 1981.

Wagner, Rudolph F. *Dyslexia and Your Child*. Rev. ed. New York: Harper & Row, 1979.

Waldman, John. *Rapid Reading Made Simple*. 2nd ed. Garden City: Doubleday, 1981.

Weaver, Constance. *Reading Process and Practice*. Portsmouth: Heinemann, 1988.

What Works: Research about Teaching and Learning. Washington: U.S. Dept. of Education, 1986.

Williams, C. K. *Flesh and Blood*. New York: Farrar, Straus & Giroux, 1987.

Williams, Emmett, ed. *An Anthology of Concrete Poetry*. New York: Something Else Press, 1967.

Wye, Margaret Enright. *The Complete Guide to Punctuation*. Englewood Cliffs: Prentice-Hall, 1985.

Index

Act of Reading, 60, 108
Aeschuylus, 59
Allen, Woody, and intentional
  mistranslation, 96
Amnesia, 68
anticipation, in reading, 49–52
Antin, David, and skytyping, 148
Antlers in the Treetops, 112
Apollinaire, Guillaume, as modernist, 125,
  126, 147
Ariosto, 30
Aristotle, 39, 59, 124
Arkin, Mort, 143, 144
"As a Wife Has a Cow," 62
Asbury-Oliver, Suzanne, 142
Ashbery, John, 39, 70, 80, 106, 112,
  117–118
Aurelius, Marcus, soothing effect of, 88
Autobiography of Alice B. Toklas, 111

Ballad of Reading Gaol, 1
basal readers, 2, 38
Beethoven, as poor speller, 17
Before Recollection, 145
Berrigan, Ted, 59, 70, 83, 106, 112, 115
Berry, Chuck, 88
Berthoff, Ann E., 70–71
Bettelheim, Bruno, 38–41
"Betty Observed," 145
Bible, 61, 124
Black Elk Speaks, 86
Blake, William, 58
Blanchot, Maurice, 30
blank in fiction, 108–109
Bleulor, Eugen, 49
blues songs, one way to write them, 61–62
Bob, Son of Battle, 24
book design, its effect on readers, 133–137
Book of Disquiet, 4
Bookmaking, 133
books as authoritative, 4–5
Bornstein, Diane, 105
Brainard, Joe, 4n, 98, 99–103
branching novels, 67–68
Braudel, Fernand, 86
Burma Shave signs, 147

Burroughs, William S., 74–75, 78–79,
  81–82, 83, 88, 96
But I Digress, 146

Cameron, Captain Allen J., 142
Campbell, Wilhelmina, 59
Candide, 132
Capote, Truman, voice of, 116
Carroll, Lewis, and cut-ups, 83
CD-ROMs, 146–147
Céline, Louis-Ferdinand, 89
Cendrars, Blaise, 7, 125
Cent mille milliards de poèmes, 69
Césaire, Aimé, 129–130
Chain of Chance, 65
Chall, Jeanne, xiv, 10, 70, 122
Chan, Charlie, stereotype of, 112
Chandler, Raymond, 89
Charlotte's Web, 22
Chaucer, Geoffrey, 125
Cherry, 98, 99–103
children's literature, 22
Clear the Range, 59
"closed" system of teaching reading and
  writing, xiv
Clough, Harold, 124
"Cocktails for Two," and incongruity,
  113–114
column confusion, 54–55, 74–80
Complete Guide to Punctuation, 145
Composition #1, and random
  permutations, 69
Critical Inquiry, 148
Crowder, Robert G., 87
cummings, e. e., and typography, 125
cut-ups, 81–82, 146

Dada poets, and chance and sound poetry,
  125
Dancing Bees, 147
day toning (reading technique), 87–89
de Vree, Paul, 120–121
Death on the Installment Plan, 89
Denby, Edwin, 42, 118, 131
Department of Education, U.S., 138

"Detached Thoughts on Books and
    Reading," 147
"Dick and Jane," 8–10
Dickens, Charles, 68
Dickinson, Emily, voice of, 112
Dietrich, Marlene, 113
Disch, Thomas M., 68
Dixon, Franklin W., 67
Documentaries, 125
Doman, Glen J., 145
Doppler Effect, corollary of in reading, 140
Dos Passos, John, 82
Drew, Carson, 17
Drew, Nancy, 67–68
Duchamp, Marcel, 82
Duck, Donald, 113
dueling books (reading technique), 86–87
duets (reading technique), 118
Dungeons and Dragons, and branching
    novels, 68
Dyslexia and Your Child, 145

Edgar, Christopher, 145
edge blur, in reading, 52, 65–66
Educating the Imagination, 145
Eliot, T. S., 81, 112, 116
Emerson, Ralph Waldo, 56
English, the irregularity of, 1–2
"Estrennes," 108
Euripides, 59
eye–mind split, in reading, 53–54, 72–74

Far Cry from Kensington, as origin of
    blank page reading technique, 107
Farrell, Kate, 147
Fear and Trembling, as difficult, 29
"Fern Hill," 117
"Fine Furs," 148
Finnegans Wake, 90, 112, 125
Fitzgerald, F. Scott, 87
fixation (in reading), 43
fold-ins (reading technique), 83–85
foreign languages, 104–105
form letters, 134–135
fotonovellas, 96–98
Foundations of Literacy, 145
Freud, Sigmund, 48, 49
Frisch, Karl von, 147
Futurists, Italian, and innovative
    typography, 125

Galbraith, John Kenneth, 138
Gallup, Dickie, 26
Genesis of Secrecy, 146
Ginsberg, Allen, 26, 117
Glaucon, 39
Golden Bowl, 112
Goodman, Ken, and reading miscues, 40
Gould, Glenn, and innovation, 141
Gray and Monroe, 11
Gray, William S., 10
Great Balls of Fire, 45
Green, Henry, and intentional mishearing,
    47–48
Grigson, Geoffrey, 83

Hardy Boys, 67–68
Hemingway, Ernest, voice of, 112
Higgins, Dick, 3
Holdaway, Don, 145
Hoover, Paul, 46
Hopper, Hedda, 28
House Beautiful, 28
Hovious, Carol, 139
How I Wrote Certain of My Books, 146
How to Teach Your Baby to Read, 145
"Hunger Artist," 87

Implied Reader, 108
intention of author, 39–40
Iser, Wolfgang, 60, 68, 73, 108
"It's Raining," 126

James, Henry, and voice, 112
Jealousy, 72
Jones, Spike, his use of the incongruous,
    113–114
Joy of Cooking, 87
Joyce, James, 90, 108, 112, 114, 125
jumping a line (reading technique), 48, 61

Kafka, Franz, 40, 87
Kierkegaard, Søren, 29
Keene, Carolyn, 67
Kermode, Frank, 47, 146
Kerouac, Jack, 26, 88
Koch, Kenneth, 90, 118, 146, 147

LaBerge, Stephen, and lucid dreaming, 90
Lamb, Charles, 132, 147
Lassie, 24
Last Year at Marienbad, 72
Lauterbach, Anne, 145
Learning to Read, 10
Leaves of Grass, 112
Lee and Allen, xiv
Lee, Marshall, on book design, 133,
    135-136, 137
Leites, Edmund, 88
Lem, Stanislaw, 65
Lemaire, Gérard-Georges, 82
Lennard, John, 146
Leonard, Elmore, 87, 114, 130
Library That Would Not Die, 1n
Lincoln, Abraham, 65
Lindbergh, Charles, 142
Lindsay, Vachel, and poetry readings, 117
linguistics approach to teaching reading, 2
listening, 122
Living Well Is the Best Revenge, 87
Loewinsohn, Ron, 120
Lone Ranger, 114
Lone Ranger and the Lost City of Gold, 24
"look-say" (word recognition) approach to
    teaching reading, 2, 10
looping a line (reading technique), 49
lucid dreaming, 90
Lupton, Ellen, on the history of the
    alphabet, 145

McDaniel, Hattie, voice of, 113
McKay, Namah, 128
McKenna, Siobhan, voice of, 114
Magic Mountain, 87
Mallarmé, Stéphane, and use of
    typography, 124
Mann, Thomas, 87
Marinetti, Filippo Tommaso, and use of
    typography, 127
Marx, Groucho, ix
mastery, the idea of, in instruction, 2
"Meet the Press," 138
megaphone (reading technique), 120-121
Merz, and use of typography, 125
Mickey Mantle Story, 24-25
Midsummer Night's Dream, 116
Millay, Edna St. Vincent, voice of, 117
mindfulness, 54, 55
mishearing, 47-48

misreading, intentional, 41
mistakes in reading, visual, 42-55
MIT Media Lab, and electronic
    newspapers, 81
Moby-Dick, 147
"Monday Rue Christine," 125
Money, 138
Monopoly, 1
Montaigne, 29-30
Moore, Clayton (The Lone Ranger), 24
Moore, Gary, 110
Morgenstern, Christian, 124
Motor Maids across the Continent, 59
Murphy, Gerald and Sara, 87
My Weekly Reader, 22-23
"Myself!", 128

Nation, 79
Nation at Risk, xv
Navratilova, Martina, 79
Nell, Victor, 132
New & Selected Poems, 147
"New Impressions of Africa," 69
New York Times, 48, 61, 75-80
New York Times Book Review, 35
New Yorker, 148
newspapers, 79-81; electronic, 81
National Center for Education Statistics, xiv
National Commission on Excellence in
    Education, xiv
"Night Song," 124
night toning (reading technique), 90
Nihil: Rien, 108, 146
Nineteen Elastic Poems, 125
Notebook of a Return to the Native Land,
    129

Odier, Daniel, 79, 81, 96
O'Hara, Frank, 115
Old Man and the Sea, 132
Ollivant, Alfred, 24
"On Cannibalism," 30
On Learning to Read, 38-41
On the Road, 88, 129
One Hundred Trillion Poems, 69
"open" system of teaching reading and
    writing, xiv
Orlando Furioso, 30
Oulipo, and use of chance operations, 60
Oz books, 22

Padgett, Ron, 45, 115, 145
page repeats (reading technique), 52-53, 71-72
page skips (reading technique), 41, 52, 66-69, 70
pantoum, 71
Paradise Lost, 116
parentheses (multiple), 69-70
Paris Review
　Henry Green interview, 47
　William Burroughs interview, 79, 89, 146
"Parole in libertà," 125, 127
Pater, Walter, 73
penmanship, 11-12; of founding fathers, 12
Pepsi Cola, 142
permutations, random, 69
Pessoa, Fernando, 4
phonics, 2, 10
Picasso, Pablo, 80
Pig Farming, 28
Pillow Book, 112
Pimp, 87
Poe, Edgar Allan, 114
"Poeta Fit, non Nascitur," 83
Poseidon Adventure, 132
Pound, Ezra
　voice of, 118
　and "The Waste Land," 146
Price, Vincent, voice of, 114
"Printed Word and Beyond," 146
Proust, Marcel, voice of, 114
"Psychopathology of Everyday Life," 48
punctuation, history of, 12, 145
Pym, Barbara, 130

Queneau, Raymond, and permutations, 69
Quiet American, 88

readability of a page, 135-136
reading
　after formal instruction, 35-37
　aloud, 110-111, 123
　alternate lines, 61
　anticipation in, 50-52
　as passive activity, 3
　at school, 33-35
　backwards, 70-71, 146
　before formal instruction, 7-8, 31-33
　blank pages, 106-108
　effect of metabolism on, 136, 138

　escapist, 130
　in cars and trains, 129
　in cities, 131-132
　in nature, 131, 147
　modern literature, 124-127
　slowly, 123
　vertically, 43-44
　while asleep, 90-91
　while walking, 130
"reading" a painting, 44
Reading As It Was, 1n
reading instruction, 2
"Reading Proust," 114-115
reading research, 2-3
reading test scores, xiv
"reading wheel," 25
Reading without Nonsense, 51
reading-writing connection, xiii-xiv, 11
readings, choral, 118-120
readings, public, by authors, 117-118
Reagan, Nancy, 78
Remembrance of Things Past, 114
Rimbaud, Arthur, 28
Robbe-Grillet, Alain, and repetition, 72, 88
Rodari, Gianni, and cut-ups, 82
Rolle, Richard, 105
Rorschach test, 83
Rosenblatt, Louise, 3
Roussel, Raymond, and use of multiple parentheses, 69, 146
"Row, Row, Row Your Boat," 118
Ruth, Babe, 48
regression, in reading, 43
repetition, 45, 61-62
Ripley's Believe It or Not 50th Anniversary Edition, 146
"rivers" (typographical), 65
Rosie O'Grady's Flying Circus, 142
Rowsome, Frank, 147

S + 7, 60
saccade, 43
Sanders, George, 28
Santa Claus, 52
Sappora, Marc, and use of random arrangements of text, 69
Saroyan, Aram, and blank pages, 108
Satie, Erik, 28
Savage, Major John S., 141
scanning a new book, 57
Schneeman, George, 80
school library, problems with, 25

Schwitters, Kurt, 125
Season in Hell, 28
Secret of the Knight's Sword, 67–68
Seeds, 85
Sesame Street, 31
Shakespeare, spelling of, 12
Shaw, George Bernard, as poor speller, 17
Shonagon, Sei, 112
sign language and dance, 147
Silverheels, Jay (Tonto), 24, 114
single word errors, 46–48, 58–61
"Skaters," 112
Skytypers East, 142, 143
Skytypers West, 142, 143, 148
skytyping, 144
skywriting, 141–144, 147, 148
Slim, Iceberg, 87
"slots" (reading technique), 85–86
Smith, Frank, 51
Song of Caedmon, 105
Song of Solomon, 1
Sonnets, 106, 112
sound off, watching TV with, 96
Spark, Muriel, 107
spelling
    changes in, 12–13
    instruction, 17–22
Stages of Reading Development, 122
Stein, Gertrude, 45, 62, 111, 117, 125
Steinbergh, Judith, 147
stencils, 91–96
Sterne, Laurence, 108
Stevens, Wallace, 115, 117
Stinis, Anthony ("Andy"), 142, 144
Stinis, Greg, 142, 143
Stokes, Katherine, 59
Striker, Fran, 24
Structures of Everyday Life, 86
subvocalization, 111, 116–117
sweep, visual, in reading, 43

Taylor, Stanford Earl, 43
Teachers & Writers Collaborative, 66
television, staccato cutting of images on,
    138–139
Tender Is the Night, 87
Tennis Court Oath, 70
Têtes de rechange, 69
Think-and-Do Book, 8–10
Thomas, Dylan, voice of, 117
Thoreau, Henry David, 131
"Throw of the Dice," 124

Times-Argus (Barre-Montpelier, Vt.), 79–80
"To Make a Dadaist Poem," 82
Tompkins, Calvin, 87
Tonto, 114
Touring Club Italiano, 129
transposing up (reading technique), 49, 62
trickle down (reading technique), 62–65
Trilling, Lionel, 115
Tristram Shandy, 108
Tulsa Kid, 115
Turner, Captain Cyril, 142
Tutu, Desmond M., 78
typefaces, 133–134
typing, as a way of reading, 106
Tzara, Tristan, 82, 83

Ulysses, 108
unconscious, role of, in reading, 38–41
Unknown Man No. 89, 87
Using Words, 17

Vanity Fair, 29
Veitch, Tom, 83, 112
Verse by the Side of the Road, 147
voice substitution, 113–116
"voice," the author's, 111–113, 146
Voyeur, 72, 88, 89

Wagner, Rudolph F., 145
Walden, 131
Waldman, John, 38, 41
Wall Street Journal, 148
"Waste Land," 81, 112
Wayne, John, voice of, 117
Weaver, Constance, 2, 40
*Webster's Ninth New Collegiate
    Dictionary*, 148
What Works, 138
What's Up, Tiger Lily?, 96
Whitman, Walt, 50, 112
whole language approach, 2, 11
Wilde, Oscar, 1
Williams, C. K., 129
Williams, William Carlos, 116
Wisher, Peter, 147
Wodehouse, P. G., 88
Wonderful Country, 88
word recognition approach ("look–say"),
    2, 10
writers-in-the-schools, 11

writing, as active, 3
"writing process," 11
Wye, Margaret Enright, 145

"Yak and Yak," 147
Yeats, William Butler, as poor speller, 17

Zelan, Karen, 38–41
"Zone," 147

Author

Photo by Patricia Padgett

RON PADGETT's books include *The Big Something*, *Great Balls of Fire*, *Ted: A Personal Memoir of Ted Berrigan*, and *Bloodwork: Selected Prose*, as well as a translation of *The Complete Poems of Blaise Cendrars* and Guillaume Apollinaire's *Poet Assassinated and Other Stories*. He has received fellowships from the Guggenheim Foundation, the National Endowment for the Arts, the New York State Council on the Arts, and the Fulbright Commission. From 1969 to 1978 he taught imaginative writing to students of all ages. For two years, Padgett directed the Saint Mark's Poetry Project in New York, before becoming publications director of Teachers & Writers Collaborative, for whom he has edited many books on the teaching of writing. For the past several years, he has also taught Imaginative Writing at Columbia University. His *New & Selected Poems* appeared in 1996.

This book was typeset in Garamond and Futura by Precision Graphics.
Typefaces used on the cover were Bodoni and Gill Sans.